GROWING WISER

Donald W. Kemper
Molly Mettler
Jim Giuffre'
Betty Matzek

Published by Healthwise, Inc. © 1986

Healthwise, Incorporated, is a nonprofit organization dedicated to helping people succeed in making positive health changes. In addition to this book, Healthwise has published the **GROWING YOUNGER Handbook**, the **HEALTHWISE Handbook** and **PATHWAYS: A Success Guide for a Healthy Life**. Videotapes and other instructional aids for health promotion and medical self-care workshops are also available. Individuals, clinics, health plans, and other organizations wishing information about Healthwise materials and handbooks should contact Healthwise directly at: P.O. Box 1989, Boise, Idaho, 83701, (208)345-1161.

Cover design and artwork by Beth Workman
Copyright © 1986, Second Edition, 1988, 1989, 1990. Healthwise, Inc., P.O. Box 1989, Boise, Idaho, 83701.

ISBN: 0-9612690-3-0
Library of Congress Catalog No.: 85-082583
Printed in the United States of America

CONTENTS

About the Authors

Donald W. Kemper is Executive Director of Healthwise and a principal designer of the *Growing Younger* and *Growing Wiser* programs. Don, who holds masters degrees in both systems engineering and public health, has co-authored four books on health promotion and presented numerous workshops and papers at health and aging conferences across the nation. Through *Growing Wiser*, Don's wisdom has started to catch up with his graying hair.

Molly Mettler, who has a master's degree in social work, is National Program Director at Healthwise and Project Director of the *Growing Wiser* program. Previously, Molly was a program planner with the Wallingford Wellness Project and coordinator of the Health Promotion With The Elderly project in Seattle. She is co-author of **A Healthy Old Age: A Sourcebook for Health Promotion with Older Adults** and has conducted numerous workshops across the USA and in England. As a result of *Growing Wiser*, Molly has learned several new jokes and her memory has improved to the point where she can remember the punch lines.

Jim Giuffre', as Associate Director of Healthwise, was a principal developer, presenter and trainer of the *Growing Younger* and *Growing Wiser* programs. Jim has a master's degree in public health education and ten years experience in designing, implementing and evaluating community and worksite health promotion programs. He has facilitated training sessions for over 3,000 older adults and for organizations in 20 states and Canada. He is co-author of **Growing Younger and Pathways**. Jim's older adult friends have him excited about new and exhilarating experiences in his 60's, 80's and his 110's. Currently, Jim is Director of the Health Department in Lewiston, Idaho.

Betty Matzek, Health Promotion Associate, has spent twenty years in various social work settings including community-based services for elders. She has been involved in every phase of the *Growing Younger* and *Growing Wiser* programs and is enthusiastic about wellness for older people. She believes that a sound mind in a sound body depends a little on your ancestors but much more on yourself and the people around you. Betty celebrated her sixtieth birthday by going on a hot air balloon ride.

Acknowledgments

The authors of *Growing Wiser* do hereby acknowledge: we were not wise enough to write this book alone. *Growing Wiser* came into being largely through the efforts and guidance of our committee members who coaxed and cajoled the program into a celebration of aging. Our thanks and appreciation go to those who served:

Steering Committee	Health Advice Committee	Public Awareness Committee
Ann Burr, RN, MA, Co-Chair	Barry J. Cusack, MD	Mary Brown
Margaret Burris, Co-Chair	Robert S. Fiedler, ACSW	Mac Browning
Goldah Anderson	Jayne Jones	Lorraine Cook
Bob Hager	Verlene Kaiser, RNP	Pat Davis
Bill Hart	Mary Lou Long, RNC, MSN	Mary Jenkins
Mary Ann Hart	Susan Madacsi, RPT	Wes Kelley
Donald Lathrop, MD	Susan McDermott, RNC, MPH	
Ruth Poindexter, RN, MA	Mark Spofford, PhD	
Pat Raino	Tom Young, MD	

Linda Aeder, Annette Park and Kathryn Jenison deserve warm thanks for their efforts in making *Growing Wiser* come alive. To our families, friends and co-workers, special appreciation is due for the support they gave us.

Special thanks go to these patient and courageous people: James B. DeLong, MSW, for his sage advice and practical suggestions; Betty Lou Donnelley for her orderly eye and publishing expertise; and Beth Workman for her fine artwork and good humor. Their collective vision and commitment to excellence is invaluable.

Good ideas usually take money to move from concept to reality. The reality for this book and the *Growing Wiser* program was made possible by financial support from the Fred Meyer Charitable Trust. Marty Lemke of the Trust added enthusiastic support and encouragement throughout *Growing Wiser's* development. Most importantly, we would like to acknowledge the exceptional people who continue to guide us along this path: the older adults who believe in *Growing Wiser*.

Words to the Wise

Growing Wiser is inspired by, created for, and dedicated to older people everywhere who continue to expand and exercise their mental vitality. *Growing Wiser* can help you to improve your memory, extend your mental alertness, strengthen your ability to accept loss and take action to assure that your home environment and independence will be protected.

By reading this book and practicing the exercises and activities described within it, you will grow wiser—not through the discovery of any magical cure for aging, but by calling forth the sage within you. *Growing Wiser* will help you to recognize the wisdom of your experience and to use it for improving the quality of your life and the world in which you live.

Most of all, *Growing Wiser* will help you feel good about yourself. It will give you a sense of celebration and dispel the myths of aging that become true only when you begin to believe them. *Growing Wiser* is a gift to yourself. Open it with great expectations and show it off to all you meet. Growing wiser is a natural process. This book will help you let it happen.

Chapter 1

On Becoming A Sage:
The Growing Wiser Formula

> *What lies behind us and what lies before us are small matters compared to what lies within us.*
> *Ralph Waldo Emerson*

Why is it that some people grow wiser and more sage-like as they age, while others experience mental decline? The *Growing Wiser* Handbook will help you answer that question for yourself and increase your chances of a mentally vital old age.

Most people grow wiser as they age. Most gain insights from their experiences and a greater understanding of what is truly important. Gaining wisdom with age is a natural process. Cultures the world over recognize the sage qualities of their elders. However, although growing wiser is part of the natural aging process, it is not inevitable. Barriers to wisdom are present at all stages of life and old age brings no exception. Growing wiser happens naturally, but not always automatically.

The best way to ensure the growth of your wisdom is to recognize and encourage the sage already within you. A sage is a wise advisor who is honored for his or her experience and perspective. Each person has such a sage within them. For some, that sage may be hard to recognize. It may be so well hidden by myths and negative expectations about aging that it is rarely allowed to speak. For others, the sage may be very present and recognizable in everything they say and do.

Growing Wiser will help you recognize, encourage and nourish the sage within you. While there is no one way to guarantee or maximize your wisdom, a standard formula for pursuing wisdom and mental alertness can be extremely helpful. *Growing Wiser* offers this.

Through using the *Growing Wiser* Formula consistently as you face the opportunities and crises of aging, you will be able to turn each new challenge toward your favor. The formula will help you stay in control of your life and keep your self-esteem high and your mind alert.

The *Growing Wiser* Formula consists of four steps. Each step may seem simple, but each represents a

key element that is often missing in the pursuit of wisdom and well-being. The *Growing Wiser* Handbook is devoted to this approach. A summary is provided below:

Step One:
Understand the facts

The first step in the *Growing Wiser* Formula is to separate what you think or are told about aging into three categories: positive facts, negative facts, and uncertainties. Too often in approaching issues involving old age, people focus only on the negative. The positive facts are ignored and the negative uncertainties are exaggerated until they seem like facts. By consciously looking at each challenge, you will be able to keep the issue in its proper perspective.

Step Two:
Reject unnecessary limitations

The second step is to carefully probe the uncertainties identified in Step One. If you cannot prove a negative assumption which limits your life, call it a myth and reject it. You can, for example, accept the negative fact that you have arthritis while rejecting the idea that it will limit your activity. Our legal system assumes that people are innocent until proven otherwise. You should give yourself the same benefit of the doubt.

Step Three:
Create positive expectations

The most important factor in whether you grow wiser is whether you expect to grow wiser. The most important factor in how well your memory works is how well you expect it to work. The most important factor in how healthy you will be is how healthy you expect to be.

Expectations are the most powerful drugs the human body has. If you replace the unnecessary limitations of Step Two with positive expectations of the future, your tomorrows are likely to be much brighter.

Step Four:
Develop an action plan

A good understanding of the situation and positive expectations for the future will enhance the quality of your life. However, they are not enough. An action plan is needed to help make those expectations happen. An action plan will put you in control of the events which affect you and will help you get what you want and expect out of life.

In the next pages these steps are discussed in greater detail. Study them and apply them to your own situation. You will find the *Growing Wiser* Formula enormously helpful in dealing with the challenges of aging.

Step One:
Understand the facts

> *God, grant me grace to accept with serenity the things that cannot be changed, courage to change the things that should be changed and wisdom to distinguish the one from the other.*
>
> *Reinhold Niebuhr*

Good news, bad news and poor reporting

An important key to growing wiser is learning to accept those things that cannot be changed. Separating what can be changed from what cannot is no easy task but equally important. The first step of the *Growing Wiser* Formula addresses that task. What really are "the facts"?

Some good news; Some bad news

Bill and Dan were retired baseball players who still loved the game. They would talk for hours both about the good old days and about the possibility that there would be baseball in heaven. A week after Dan died, Bill was walking in his garden when he heard Dan's voice. "Bill," the wise voice said, "I have some good news and some bad news. The good news is there is baseball in heaven— we play every afternoon. The bad news is you're scheduled to pitch on Friday."

Life is full of good news and bad news. Some news turns out to be true and some to be false. When you believe any piece of information about you, there are four possibilities as shown below:

Good news that is true

"You have just won the Reader's Digest Sweepstakes!" Good news, if it is true, can be four star material. If a piece of information about you is true and if it is good, it can do nothing but help you feel good and stay healthy.

Good news that is not true

"You actually only won the $5 consolation prize." Good news that turns out to be false brings a mixed blessing. As long as you think it is true, you may experience good feelings. Only when you learn the truth do you lose that feeling. Still, little harm is usually done.

Bad news that is true

"You owe $10,000 in back taxes." If it is true, there is little good to say about bad news. It gives you bad feelings right from the start. All you can do is to accept it, deal with it, sometimes grow from it, and move on to something else.

Bad news that is not true

"The IRS thinks you owe $10,000 more in taxes." Bad news, falsely thought to be true, can be just as debilitating as if it were true. The fear of some bad event can cause as many problems as the bad news itself.

Separating fact from fiction

Your first task in developing the sage within you is to learn to tell fact from fiction—particularly where bad news is concerned. If you err by falsely believing in good news, the consequences are usually light—that is why optimists do so well in life.

> *Too much of a good thing is wonderful.*
>
> *Mae West*

Positive Facts

The sage is just as aware of positive facts as he is of negative ones. Often, it is only through the good news of life that myths and limitations are debunked. Whenever you are faced with a tough situation, stop to take stock in yourself. If you forget a friend's name at a party and are feeling kind of stupid, recognize that you remembered the names of ten or twenty others or that you can still tell a terrific story—this is proof enough that your memory is basically good. If you are fretting because you need help to fix up your house, remember that you can still make a great cherry pie or bring a smile to a grandchild's face. Always assume the best in and for yourself.

Positive facts are so easily ignored

that it is important to display them prominently for both yourself and others to see. If you walk a mile a day, or sing in the church choir, or volunteer for a good cause, show pride in yourself. By fully understanding all of the good things in your life, every challenge of aging will be more easily met.

Negative Facts

When you hear bad news that checks out to be 100 percent true, there is nothing you can do except try to accept it. Negative facts are plentiful, particularly in the later years of life. For example, you may lose your vision or at least part of it; or you may, at some point, need help to fix your meals. Accept only negative facts that are clearly shown to be true. All other negative information should be rejected as unproven until shown otherwise.

The best way to determine if negative information is true is to ask questions, and avoid assumptions. Suppose you are told you have cancer. Ask yourself, your doctor and any other source you trust:

- Are you sure it is I? (Any chance you have the wrong chart?)

- Could you have made an error? Is the test sometimes wrong? Should I get a second opinion?

• What are the chances that it will heal itself on its own? Are any such cures described in medical journals? If so, what can I do to improve my chances?

• How can I get rid of it—or keep it from getting worse?

• How can I live with it with as little effect on my daily activities as possible?

Accept only those answers with which you are satisfied. Probe every restriction or limitation placed upon you. Ask why you should be hospitalized when you prefer to be home, or why you can't continue to work in the garden if that is what you like to do. The more you control the negative news and eliminate unnecessary limitations, the less dramatic its effect will be on your life.

Questionable information and other uncertainties

In trying to understand the facts of your situation, treat all unproven negative information as highly questionable. There is danger in letting negative ideas just sit around in your mind. Negative prophecies have a way of becoming self-fulfilling; if you think long enough about your memory getting worse, it probably will.

If the bad news cannot be proven beyond the shadow of a doubt, send the jury home and assume that the news was in error. Should new information come later, you can always reassess.

Understanding the facts of your situation may call for all of the skills your sage can muster. It is a task that requires great watchfulness—for friends, family and society in general often place limitations on you that may be founded on myth or poor information. It is up to you to maintain that watch and your awareness.

> *The best antidote to fear is to know all we can about a situation.*
> *John Glenn*

Step Two:
Reject unnecessary limitations

Outwardly I am 83 years old, but inwardly I am every age. At each age I am myself. During much of my life I was anxious to be what someone else wanted me to be. Now I have given up that struggle. I am what I am.

Elizabeth Coatsworth

How to avoid being myth-interpreted

*Once upon a time, a distinguished, gray-haired gentleman walked into a doctor's office for a check-up. After putting his patient through a series of tests, the doctor announced happily to his client, "You're in excellent shape for a 60-year-old!" The gentleman corrected him, "Doctor, I'm 75 years old." The doctor's jaw dropped in amazement, "75! Well, you certainly come from good, healthy stock. How old was your father when he died?" "Who said anything about my father dying? He's 95, alive and well, and out playing golf today." The doctor shook his head and asked, "Then tell me, how old was your grandfather when he died?" The gentleman raised an eyebrow quizzically, "Who said anything about Grandpa dying? He's 115 and, in fact, he's getting married tomorrow." "Married?! At his age?!" the doctor gasped, "Why on earth does he want to get married?" The gentleman looked squarely in the doctor's eye and replied, "Who said anything about Grandpa **wanting** to get married?"*

The doctor in this story "myth-interpreted" what he thought were logical assumptions about the 75-year-old man and his busy forebears. The doctor is not alone. Many people continue to operate under a veil of delusions and misinformation about aging. Myths about aging and being old abound. Here are just a few:

Myth #1
You can't teach an old dog new tricks.

Fact: Both old dogs and old people are quite good at learning new skills and information. On the other hand, you may not be able to force an old dog to do new tricks, and an older person may be reluctant to learn something new unless it has a useful application in his or her life. This apparent reluctance to learn may actually be due to applying both wisdom and intelligence to the situation.

Myth #2
Intelligence declines with age.

Fact: If health is good, there is no significant decline in intelligence with age. Although the speed of memory recall drops in most people, basic intelligence often continues to improve with age. The amount of stimulation you get from your environment and the people around you will have more influence on your intellect than your age.

Myth #3
Old people eventually become senile.

Fact: Senility, or dementia, is caused by specific diseases and health problems like Alzheimer's disease, depression, or poor nutrition. It is not a normal result of aging. The vast majority of older people remain mentally vital and alert throughout their lives.

Myth #4
Old people have to live in nursing homes.

Fact: Less than 5 percent of older people live in nursing homes or institutions. Most live independently in their own homes or with relatives.

Myth #5
Old people have no interest in sex.

Fact: Although erections may be less firm for older men and vaginal lubrication less fluid for older women, both men and women can, and do, enjoy sex and sexuality late in life.

Myth #6
You won't live long if your parents didn't.

Fact: Although there is a hereditary factor in longevity, other factors are far more important in determining how long you live. Following good fitness, nutrition and relaxation habits adds years to your life.

Myth #7
Old people can't find work.

Fact: Although attitudes often work against hiring older persons, many of these attitudes are changing. Job sharing and job restructuring are increasing the opportunity for older workers. Older workers have higher productivity and lower absenteeism than other workers.

Myth #8
Old people want to be young.

Fact: Most older people are happy to have lived their lives and are not anxious to go back. As Jonathan Swift wrote, "No wise man ever wished to be younger."

These myths seek to convince us that human beings, aged sixty-plus, magically and mysteriously become old and decrepit. According to these misconceptions, old people are expected to act their age by going slowly and surely downhill. Older adults are meant to have lots of aches and lots of pains, but no vitality and no fun. They are supposed to spend all their time talking about the good old days. If they are lucky, they will live out the rest of their days in rocking chairs; wheelchairs if they're not. These myths unfortunately have a life of their own and, repeated often enough, become true in the minds of many.

A quick glance through history books and around your neighborhood will give you a different picture of old age. Michaelangelo designed the dome of St. Peter's at age 83. Gandhi was in his seventies when he launched India's struggle for independence. Benjamin Franklin was past 80 when he helped draft the U.S. Constitution. Grandma Moses started painting at 78 and kept going for the next twenty-three years. The artist Georgia O'Keeffe, after becoming blind, learned to do pottery in her nineties.

"Whoa there," you say, "What about me? I'm no Grandma Moses." A productive and exciting old age is not reserved just for the superstars of art, literature and politics. The average person, too, has a large capacity for achievement in old age. Thousands of older people give lie to the notion that aging is a nowhere prop-

osition. You, too, can reject age prejudice and any unnecessary limitations that others may place on you.

Step Two of the *Growing Wiser* Formula calls upon you to reject any unnecessary limitations and self-defeating messages that come your way. Myths about getting old only serve to squelch the sage within you. Refuse to be suppressed!

> *As the cells in my body renew*
> *And my purpose in life I review*
> *I find growing older*
> *I'm now growing bolder*
> *And increasingly hard to subdue!*
> *Helen G. Ansley*

How to fight back, stand ground and move ahead.

- **Know the facts.**
  The myths of aging are based upon fear and folklore and need to be dispelled by information and truth. Use this handbook, other good books on aging and your own wisdom to help you replace fiction with fact.

- **Be assertive.**
  Stand up for yourself and courteously command the respect you deserve. If you feel you need a little practice first, turn to page 96 for some helpful guidelines.

- **Be bloody-minded.**
  This is a British term which com-

bines the best of feistiness and nail-spitting cussedness into a heroic package. Winston Churchill was bloody-minded, Caspar Milquetoast is not. Alex Comfort, the English gerontologist, writes, "Bloody-mindedness is an index of self-respect, and the most bloody-minded, in that they speak also on behalf of others who are timid, are often the gentlest and most principled. Bloody-minded people act on their conscience."

- **Believe in yourself.**
  Have great expectations. The best is yet to be.

Step Three:
Create positive expectations

Whether you believe you can do a thing or not, you are right.
  Henry Ford

Mind over matter: What you think is what you get

In 1964, a magazine editor named Norman Cousins came down with a very rare and sometimes fatal illness called ankylosing spondylitis. The specialists attending him gave Cousins a one in five hundred chance of recovering from the illness. At that low point, Cousins devised a plan to cure himself. With his doctor as a willing partner, he successfully overcame his illness by combining high doses of Vitamin C with plenty of hope, laughter and an enormous will to live. Cousins wrote about his experience in a book which has already become a classic, **The Anatomy of an Illness.** In his book, Cousins describes the powerful and mysterious relationship between mind and body. His experience convinced him that attitudes, beliefs and emotions have a profound effect on physical and mental well-being.

You have heard of psychosomatic illness—when a person "thinks" himself into being sick. Evidence now supports the idea of psychosomatic "wellness." For sickness and for health, what you think **is** what you get. Step Three of the *Growing Wiser* Formula is about getting the most from your mind and body through positive expectations.

The drug store inside your brain

Medical science is making some remarkable discoveries about your brain. Your gray matter not only holds the key to your consciousness, your memory, your dreams and stories; it also holds the key to an internal drug store. Researchers have found that the brain is, among other things, a huge gland which produces a number of substances that help you to better health. Your brain creates natural painkillers called endorphins, gammaglobulin for fortifying your immune system, and interferon for combatting infections, viruses, even cancer.

Your brain can combine these and other substances into a vast number of tailor-made "prescriptions" for what ails you. Whether the pharmacy in your brain is open for business depends largely upon you. Your ability to heal yourself is hooked onto your belief system. Your expectations of what could happen, whether they are positive or negative, affect what goes on inside your body. In other words, your body (**and mind**) follows the path of its expectations.

Long before my own serious illness I became convinced that creativity, the will to live, hope, faith and love have biochemical significance and contribute strongly to healing and to well-being. The positive emotions are life-giving experiences.

Norman Cousins

Great and not-so-great expectations

Life can have the uncanny knack of turning out just like you expect it to. Perhaps you have heard the term "self-fulfilling prophecy." When you make a prediction, either good or bad about yourself, other people or an event, you tend to behave as if it is true. Often, without being completely aware of what you are doing, you bring about the expected result. In this regard, expectations are both a problem and a promise. They are a problem when they cause a person to believe in the worst possible outcome.

At a high school football game in California, four people went to the first aid station complaining of severe stomach upset. In fact, they showed all the symptoms of food poisoning. The doctor on duty discovered that each of them had purchased a soft drink from one particular machine under the stands. Acting with what he thought to be justifiable caution, the doctor took two steps in the direction of preven-tion: he issued an order to turn off the soda dispenser and he made an announcement to the rest of the crowd to warn them that there had been some cases of food poisoning and to stay away from that particular machine.

Immediately following the announcement hundreds of football fans were stricken with symptoms of food poisoning. Ambulances from five hospitals rushed back and forth to the stadium. Several people with severe symptoms had to be hospitalized. Meanwhile, back at the stadium, it was soon determined that the soft drinks had nothing to do with the illness. Another announcement was made and the ailing fans recovered as quickly as they had become ill. Those who had fallen ill upon hearing the first announcement had fallen prey to their own negative expectations.

Words and expectations also play a positive role. Dr. Kenneth Pelletier, in his book **Longevity,** writes of an experiment in a nursing home which demonstrated the power of positive expectations. In this case the experiment showed that what others expect of you has an impact on what you may or may not achieve.

The nursing home residents were divided into two groups and each resident was given a small plant. One group was told that they would be responsible for taking care of and watering their plants. The other group was told that the nursing home staff would look after their plants for them.

Taking care of a plant may not seem like much in the scheme of things, but the results of the experiment proved otherwise. The residents who watered their own plants became more alert and socially active and, amazingly, their mortality rate was half that of the patients who only watched their plants get watered!

The nurses were affected also. As they began to notice improvements in the residents that looked after their plants, the nurses began to raise their expectations of those residents. This, too, had a positive effect on their overall health.

Words, thoughts, hopes, beliefs and expectations are as powerful as any drug. For the football fans, simple words had changed an afternoon sporting event into a scene of panic and mass hysteria. For the residents at the nursing home the control over one plant and the raised expectations of the nurses who looked after them made a difference between life and death.

Expectations and positive mental programming

What goes on inside your mind has a strong influence on your physical and mental health. No one knows why precisely, but the fact is real: what you think has a great deal to do with what happens to you.

Consider expectations about old age. If you believe that growing old means growing wise and that getting older means getting better, chances are you will continue to live a productive, joyous and enriching life. Your thoughts will influence your actions in a way that will make the event more likely to happen. Facing a challenge or a goal with raised expectations will help you handle the situation as best you can.

To gain control over what goes on inside your mind you need to look at how you view yourself and what kinds of mental pictures and self-talk go along with your thoughts.

> *The mind in its own place and in itself can make a heaven of hell and a hell of heaven.*
> *John Milton*

Self esteem: The importance of liking yourself

What do you see when you look into a mirror? Do you concentrate solely on the wrinkles, the thinning hair, the bags under your eyes? Or do you see laugh lines which reflect a lifetime of smiles, chuckles and a positive outlook? Do you see a light in your eyes that tells of the wisdom and depth which comes from meeting life head-on? The ability to look into a mirror and like the person who looks back is key to creating positive expectations and high well-being.

People with low self-esteem think of themselves as incapable, unlovable, unworthy. Not trusting in their own abilities, they let others do their thinking and talking for them. They often feel victimized and pushed around. This makes them angry, but they don't express either their rage or frustration. With bottled-up emotions and riddled with self-doubt, they suffer from depression, anxiety and high levels of stress. A person with low self-esteem has expectations all right, but those expectations are negative and lackluster; life holds little promise or joy.

In contrast, people with positive self-regard consider themselves capable, competent and deserving. They have a sense of control over their lives. They trust their decisions and judgments. They look at themselves realistically, feeling good about their strengths and taking their weaknesses in stride. They do not feel any need to manipulate or dominate other people, nor do they let others control them. They appreciate and like compliments, but their self-esteem does not depend upon approval from others. Their expectations are positive and expansive. They embrace life, laughter and love.

It is possible that you fall some-where in between self-hate and self-adoration. Most people do. It is not uncommon for a person to feel competent, worthy and capable in one situation, for example on the home front, and anxious and uncomfortable in another setting.

Perhaps your self-esteem is beginning to be affected by the messages you are picking up from others regarding your age. ("You're slowing down, better take it easy.") If this is the case, take heart. Your sense of self never stops growing. Your personality is not etched in stone. Although you cannot undo the past, it is within your power and capability to make the most of today and tomorrow.

There are two things you can do **right now** to boost and nurture your self-esteem and pave the way for positive expectations:

- Become better acquainted with the power of imagination

- Learn to say nice things to and about yourself

The power of imagination: Mental imagery

Mental pictures produce responses in your body. This doesn't mean that if you think of the sun, you'll get a suntan, but rather, your body will react internally. Try this quick experiment: close your eyes and imagine that you are holding a lemon wedge in your hand. Feel the smooth, slightly oily skin of the lemon on your fingers. Bring the lemon to your nose and deeply inhale its fragrance. Now picture yourself biting down hard into the lemon. Your mouth puckers in response to the lemon's acid tartness. Open your eyes; the lemon is imaginary but it produces just as much saliva as a real lemon.

The memory of a sad time can bring tears and the recollection of a past pleasure can generate good feelings. You can even slow down your heartbeat by thinking about it. The pictures may be "in your head," but the responses to the pictures are very real.

Consciously creating mental pictures is called *visualization*. This technique has been successfully used to treat stress disorders and serious illnesses such as cancer. Turn to page 20 for a simple visualization technique that you can practice.

Self-talk

Mental pictures are usually accompanied by verbal messages to yourself. Self-talk, like mental imagery, is what your subconscious mind goes to work on. You are telling your mind what to do when you give yourself messages like "I can never remember names" or "Boy, my memory is really failing." The result?

You can't remember names because in effect you are programming yourself not to.

As with visualization and mental images, you can train yourself to replace negative messages with positive self-talk or *affirmations*. An affirmation is a phrase that sends strong, positive statements to the subconscious. It is a method of "making firm" that which you are imagining. Positive affirmations allow you to raise expectations about life and, in consequence, change and improve the reality you create for yourself. A step-by-step guide to creating positive affirmations is on page 22.

Great expectations and beyond

More and more, medical science is uncovering the mysterious link between mind and body. The sage within you is in possession of vast powers, powers which are only now being charted. These powers are vitally linked to your expectations. Good or bad, your expectations shape your life. Make the most of them.

> *Grow old along with me*
> *The best is yet to be,*
> *The last of life*
> *For which the first was made.*
> *Robert Browning*

Step four:
Develop an action plan

> *I hear and I forget*
> *I see and I remember*
> *I do and I understand.*
> *Chinese proverb*

This proverb embraces the essence of the *Growing Wiser* Formula. While it is critically important that you **hear** and understand the facts, **see** and reject unnecessary limitations, it is the **doing** that counts the most. The doing involves creating positive expectations and then developing a plan to move from expectations to action.

Taking action puts you in the driver's seat. Any specific action in response to a situation or crisis is probably less important than the process of doing something. You gain a sense of control when you take the helm for decisions and choices. Even if the decision or action turns out to be less than perfect, the process of getting "down to it" gives you an opportunity to identify and reflect your rights, values and feelings.

Consider the alternative. If you do not take action, you lose both control and power. Actions are done to you rather than your doing the acting. In essence, you give up your rights, values and feelings. Making decisions and developing action plans will allow you to remain in control and be in charge of your personal well-being. This is the ultimate quality of a sage.

A woman in her eighties recently visited her doctor seeking treatment advice for a painfully arthritic right knee. The physician conducted a brief examination of the knee and upon finishing commented, "There is nothing medically wrong with this knee. The pain you feel is normal. What do you expect from an eighty-year-old knee?" The woman eyeballed the doctor for several moments and in her firmest voice said, "Doctor, I expect it to feel just like my left knee. It's eighty years old, too. Now what advice would you give a 40-year-old complaining of the same pain?"

Here we have a classic case of an older woman, a sage indeed, whose assertiveness and bias for action prevented any compromising of her rights as a patient and her values and feelings as a competent, confident older adult. The sage within you also has a bias for action. Awaken it if it has been dormant. Shake it loose. Nourish it if it is already blossoming. Take action! Right or wrong, it is the only way to move ahead.

> *Don't just stand there, do something!*
> *Mom*

Characteristics of a successful action plan

Now that the case has been made for taking control and taking action, how do you do it? You have already been doing it for a good many years in raising a family, working at a job, and nurturing your personal and career development.

Developing and carrying out successful action plans is more an art than a science. It demands good planning and communication skills —sage talents which you may already possess. What follows are characteristics of a successful action plan which will bring out the best of the sage within you.

1. **The plan addresses a goal.**
   If you can "see" the target, you are more likely to hit it.

2. **It reflects your review of all available options.**
   By looking at alternatives you will strengthen your confidence in the final plan.

3. **You can visualize accomplishing it.**
   If you can "see" yourself doing it, it is much easier to make it happen.

4. **It is easy to start.**
   The first steps of the action plan should be easy "warm-up" activities to build your confidence.

5. **It recognizes the challenges.**
   By predicting what barriers may arise, you can plan to overcome them.

6. **It includes rewards.**
   A good plan has built-in celebrations at each stage of success.

7. **It encourages support.**
   Support from friends and a positive environment will help any plan succeed.

8. **Its progress can be followed.**
   Good plans can be monitored by periodic feedback. It lets you know if you are on the right track.

Armed with these characteristics of an action plan success, you are sure to be 100 percent successful. Right? WRONG! Your timing for change is also critical. Prepare at any time for a future change, but wait until you are ready to actually make it. There are no guarantees to success, except those that you yourself provide. When you plan well and commit yourself, you almost always succeed. Go forth. Create an action plan and move your positive expectations into reality. May the Sage be with you!

Recommended Reading
A Good Age by Alex Comfort. New York: Crown Publishers, 1976.

Anatomy of an Illness by Norman Cousins. New York: Bantam Books, 1979.

The Healing Heart by Norman Cousins. New York: Avon Books, 1983.

Creative Visualization by Shakti Gawain. New York: Bantam Books, 1978.

The Art of Aging by Evelyn Mandel. Minneapolis: Winston Press, 1981.

Longevity by Kenneth R. Pelletier. New York: Delacorte Press, 1981.

10 Paths to Positive Expectations

It's great to have your feet on the ground, but keep them moving.
P.K. Sideliner

Rank the following "paths" 1-10 according to their importance to you at this time of your life. Write 1 beside the path that would do the most to raise your expectations. Then circle the path(s) you could start walking on today.

_____ Explore new interests.

_____ Take control of my life.

_____ Make some new friends.

_____ Lend support to a cause or campaign.

_____ Take time to think about problems and their possible solutions.

_____ Create a bright new vision of the road ahead.

_____ Find a way to reward myself daily.

_____ Make room for play.

_____ Take good care of my health.

_____ Say yes to life!

Adapted from **Aging: A New Look,** *by Alexandra Robbin, American Guidance Service.*

Me, Glorious Me

This little light of mine
I'm gonna let it shine
Every day, every way
Gonna let my little light shine.
                                Gospel song

Take a large sheet of paper and a big box of crayons or colored pencils. If you are feeling artistic, draw a picture of yourself in the center of the paper, or you can write your name. Now, with a flourish, write down:

- 5 things you do well, e.g., cooking, gardening, reading stories to your grandchildren

- 5 reasons why other people like you, e.g., responsible, thoughtful, great host, sense of humor

- 5 things you like about yourself, e.g., irrepressible, irresistible, and iridescent.

Keep on adding to the list; turn the paper over to accommodate all your good qualities. Cover 5, 10, 15 pieces of paper front and back. The finished product will be a portrait of a unique and special person. There is no one quite like you. Celebrate yourself!

Visualization: Creating positive mental pictures

Imagination is more important than knowledge.
Albert Einstein

Imagination is more than child's play. You use imagination every day in many subtle and diverse ways. You imagine the smile on your friend's face just before you drop by for a visit. Getting ready to prepare dinner involves imagination: you picture what you'll fix and how it will look on the plate.

In visualization, you use your imagination to consciously create a clear image of something you wish to make happen. Your goal may be on any level—physical, emotional, mental or spiritual. You can visualize yourself being radiantly healthy, feeling peaceful and serene or perhaps with improved memory, effort-lessly remembering the names of new acquaintances. Whatever the goal, creative visualization can help you replace negative imagery with positive mental pictures which will reduce the effects of stress in your life.

A simple exercise

1.   First, think of something you would like to have happen. If visualization is new to you, choose something simple, such as going for a walk in the sunshine or easily remembering the names of new people you meet at the senior center.

2.   Get into a comfortable position, either sitting or lying down, where you won't be disturbed. Relax your body completely. Breathe deeply and slowly from your abdomen. Feel yourself becoming deeply relaxed.

3.   In your relaxed state, begin to imagine what you want to occur. If it is a situation or event, picture yourself there and everything occurring just as you want it to. If you are visualizing good health, imagine yourself full of energy, your body strong and flexible. Treat yourself to a wide-screen, technicolor daydream in which you are the star and director.

4.   Keeping the image in mind, come up with a positive statement to your-self such as "I am very strong and healthy" or "I am feeling very relaxed and calm." This positive statement can serve as a caption to your mental picture.

Special Notes

- If doubts or other images arise, don't resist or try to prevent them. Release them with a deep breath and return to your positive image.

- Don't worry if you don't "see" a mental picture or image. Some people get very clear images, some may just think about it or have a feeling about what they are trying to imagine. Whatever works best for you is fine.

- You may "dream up" something unusual or unexpected. The best thing to do is to examine it closely and fully. ("Hmmm. Just what is this one-eyed, one-horned, flying purple people-eater?") Our fears come from things we don't confront.

- Visualize only as long as you find it fun and beneficial. This is not another "must" to add to your list of "shoulds." Your mental journey can last 5 minutes or a half hour...whatever seems right for you.

Using visualization in a creative and beneficial way can be like learning to paint with watercolors. The first time you try you may end up with all sorts of blurred lines, overlapping colors and a dripping mess. However, with practice and a spirit of adventure and exploration, you will soon be creating your own masterpieces.

Affirmations: Creating positive self-talk

I think I can, I think I can, I think I can.
from The Little Engine That Could

An affirmation is a phrase or sentence that sends strong, positive statements to you about yourself.

The practice of using affirmations allows us to create a positive blueprint upon which our subconscious mind can get to work. Positive affirmations allow us to raise our expectations about life so we can change and improve the reality we create for ourselves.

Examples of affirmations

An affirmation can be any positive statement about yourself. It can be put in very general terms:

- I am a lovable and capable person.

- I love and appreciate who I am.

Or, affirmations can be used to help you with a specific issue, such as memory, health or relationships:

- My memory serves me well.

- I am vibrantly healthy.

- My joints are strong and flexible.

- My relationship with _____ is full of love and understanding.

Guidelines for creating an affirmation

- Accentuate the positive. Put your affirmation in positive terms. Instead of saying "My sore neck hurts me less," go for a bold, assertive statement like "My neck is flexible and relaxed."

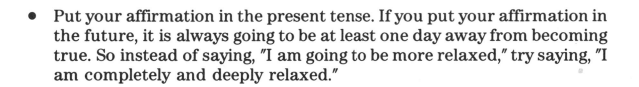

- Put your affirmation in the present tense. If you put your affirmation in the future, it is always going to be at least one day away from becoming true. So instead of saying, "I am going to be more relaxed," try saying, "I am completely and deeply relaxed."

- Make it important to you. Construct an affirmation around a topic, thought or issue which is of concern to you. If it is trivial, you won't feel inclined either consciously or subconsciously to go along with it.

- State your affirmations personally, in terms of yourself. Try not to make them oriented toward someone else. Try, "I have a full and satisfying relationship with my children," rather than "Steven and Mortimer realize how wonderful I am."

- Keep it simple. "I am happy" conveys a stronger message to your brain than "I am agreeably cheerful and take pleasure in all manner of fabulous fandangos."

Putting your affirmations to work

- Like prayers, affirmations can be repeated silently, spoken aloud, written down or even sung.

- Repeat your affirmations with all the conviction you can muster. Try to let go of your doubts and hesitation (at least for a few minutes) and put positive emotional energy into them.

- Writing your affirmations 10 to 20 times on a piece of paper can be doubly effective because you are writing and reading them at the same time. If you feel any resistance or negative thoughts about what you are writing, turn the paper over and write those, too. (For example, if your affirmation is "My memory serves me well," your doubts or negative thoughts might be "I'm too old, I'm not well and I don't care.") By recognizing your counter-affirmations, you will have an insight into some of your negative self-talk. With this in mind, think of some affirmations which will help counteract these negative beliefs.

- Say your affirmation silently or aloud while relaxing, walking, meditating, stretching, doing household chores, anywhere, anytime. Right before going to sleep and right after waking up are very good times.

- Post your affirmations in various places around your house. Your mirror, telephone, refrigerator and desk are good starting points.

- Words to the wise—affirmations are to be used in such a way that they bring increased joy and meaning to your life. Affirmations are not meant to contradict your true feelings. They are not a tool for repressing yourself. Use them wisely and constructively, to help change unconscious negative thoughts and underlying assumptions.

P.S. You are a wonderful, wise and lovable human being.

The *Growing Wiser* Formula and You

Our remedies oft in ourselves do lie.
William Shakespeare

Describe a problem or situation which concerns you: _____

_____

_____

_____

Step One: Separate the positive facts from the negative facts and any uncertainties.
See pages 4-6.

Positive Facts	Negative Facts	Uncertainties

Step Two: Identify limitations and reject any that are unnecessary. See pages 7-10.

_____

_____

_____

_____

Step Three: Creative positive expectations. How would you like the situation to be resolved?
See pages 11-15.

_____

_____

_____

_____

See pages 22-24. Your Affirmation: _____

_____

_____

Step Four: Develop an Action Plan. What are your available options for action?
See pages 16-17.

a. _____

b. _____

c. _____

Star (*) the option that seems best to you right now. Briefly describe what you see yourself doing.

_____

Describe how you will begin this week.

_____

What barriers to your plan do you anticipate?

_____

How will you celebrate each state of success?

_____

Which friend and what changes in your environment will best support your change?

_____

How will you chart your progress?

_____

Memory

The amazing memory

To hear the average person talk, the human memory may seem to be a very limited and unreliable device which is constantly letting us down and often on the verge of disintegrating entirely. People complain about their memories more than their looks. Particularly among many older adults, memory is routinely maligned.

However, based on a more objective view, it would seem that the memory's greatest fault is to let us forget how amazing it really is. It is estimated that the brain has two billion brain cells. Each cell is capable of storing a vast amount of information within. The brain's capacity to store memories is practically limitless.

Think for a moment of your first day at school. What did the school look like? How did you get there? How did you feel? Chances are you can remember at least some of that in spite of the fact that it happened years ago and that thousands of days of experience have been stored in your memory since. Your memory is far larger, far more flexible and far faster than a computer.

> *One of the most moving aspects of life is how long the deepest memories stay with us.*
> *Laurens Van Der Post*

How memory works

The human brain performs four basic memory functions: input, processing, storage and retrieval. Each function is linked to a different type of memory.

Input: Sensory memory

Everything you learn must first come through one of your senses. Vision, hearing, touch, taste or smell must be involved to receive the initial message. *Sensory memory* holds the received message for a very brief time—only a few seconds. To use visual memory as an example, look away from your book and focus on whatever is in front of you. Look at all the details. Now close your eyes for a moment and try to reconstruct the scene. You will notice the details fade fast. Auditory memory is much the same. As you listen to someone speak, you hold all of the words and tones in auditory memory only long enough to make sense of them. As little as one minute later, you may find it difficult to repeat a complete sentence correctly. The sensory memory is receiving complex messages continually throughout the day. Fortunately, only a part of it gets stored.

Processing: Primary memory

Your brain sorts through sensory messages as they come in and separates what is "interesting" to study. The interesting inputs are stored temporarily in short-term or primary memory where you can process, or think about the inputs. *Primary memory*, like sensory memory, is very short-lived, lasting no more than a few minutes. During that time, your brain again sorts through the messages, deciding what seems interesting enough to store in long-term or *secondary memory*.

Your memory can be compared to an office desk. The in-box represents your sensory memory. Everything you see, hear, touch, taste or smell must come in through the in-box to get to the desk. If the information is interesting to you, you spread it out on the desk top. Here, your primary memory takes another look at the information.

When you finish working on the information, your mind decides if you will need that information again. If not, it goes right out of primary memory and into the trash. If the information is something you want to learn, you file it away inside the desk, into your secondary, or long-term memory. This is where new information is connected to previous memories. Secondary memory lasts from a few minutes to a lifetime.

Storage and retrieval: Secondary memory

Most of your mental desk is used

for storage. The amount of information a brain can store is believed to be virtually unlimited. New information is cross-referenced so that each memory is associated with the time and place you learned it, as well as with scores of other features that link it with other memories.

When you need to remember something you have previously learned, your brain searches through your mental desk looking for the memory. The cross- references and associations you made earlier determine whether or not (and how quickly) you will find the memory.

Usually, complaints about forgetfulness are not as focused on losing something completely from memory as they are about finding the information when it is needed. You know the information—you just can't "bring it to mind" for the moment. If you were to get the right cue, it would be remembered in an instant, or if someone else were to provide the name or whatever, you would say, "of course, now why didn't I think of that?"

Good memory retrieval has relatively little to do with intelligence. Through memory training exercises, both the speed and effectiveness of memory retrieval can be increased. Try the memory improvement activities beginning on page 44.

The human memory is a wonderful, baffling thing. The enormous assortment of facts and recollections that even a 20-year-old has had stick in his mind for instant recall would fill many hundreds of volumes if written down.
David Gunston

Memory and aging

Does memory decline with age? Most people would answer yes. Yet there is no tangible proof that age alone adversely affects the memory.

Actually, older people generally experience memory reductions in only three areas:

1. On the average, older people take slightly more time to learn something new.

2. On the average, older people take slightly more time to recall memories.

3. On the average, older people are more adversely affected by distractions. That is, they remember less when there are several conversations or messages competing for attention at the same time.

There are positive facts that counterbalance those concerns.

1. Neither sensory nor primary memory declines significantly with age. If you can see or hear it, the memory can record it.

2. Little is lost from memory. With the right cues, an older person can remember just as much as a younger person.

3. An older person can concentrate better. While an older person may take more time to learn something, he or she can also focus on learning for a longer time than a younger person.

By age 60 or 70, a person has millions of memories that must be sorted through each time a new experience is filed away or a previously learned memory is retrieved. The sheer number of both the memories and the associations linking them add to the time and memory cues needed to pull out a certain memory. It also creates the opportunity for a greater memory of meanings.

It's a poor memory that only works backwards.
Lewis Carroll

Memory of meanings: The basis of wisdom

There are two primary functions of memory. The first is the direct storage and retrieval of information. As the average person ages past 70, he or she needs a little more time to store new memories and a few more cues to retrieve old ones than he or she needed at age 40 or 50. The second function of memory is to link one memory or experience with another in a way that creates new information. In this area, older adults seem to have a clear advantage over the young.

In one study, twenty school teachers aged 21-25 and twenty school teachers aged 61-70 were asked several questions which required "memory associations" to answer. For example, "What fictional horror character would starve to death in northern Sweden in the summertime?" (Answer: Dracula, because it stays light all day.) Few people have stored the answers to these questions. Rather, they have to link several memories to construct an answer.

The older teachers had scores for the test which were vastly superior to the younger teachers' scores. The results suggest that the ability to derive meaning and to create new information from existing memory improves over a lifetime.

This ability to use past experience to deal with problems that have no one correct answer is termed "crystallized intelligence." Since crystallized intelligence improves with age, it is an important aspect of growing wiser.

You may at times feel discouraged when you can't recall a person's name, a phone number or where you put your keys. Don't be too hard on yourself. Remember, as you age your memory adapts to the grander purpose of understanding more about your world.

With the ancient is wisdom, and in length of years, understanding.
Job 12:12

Causes of memory loss

While memory suffers relatively little from normal aging alone, older people are prone to a number of conditions that can create memory problems. Fortunately, most of those conditions can be both prevented and reversed.

Medications

The overuse of medications may be the single greatest cause of memory problems among older adults. Because older adults are more likely to be taking one or more medications and because many drugs stay in the older person's system longer, you should develop a healthy respect for medications. Although all medications should be suspected if symptoms of memory loss are present, those medications identified on page 58 should be reviewed with particular care and discussed with your physician.

Depression

Depression has a powerful impact on memory loss and other symptoms of dementia. Normal aging, by itself, seems to carry no increased risk of depression, but since illness and loss do often bring on depression and are more often experienced late in life, depression among older adults is a major concern. The section on Self-Care for the Blues (page 60) may be particularly useful.

Poor nutrition

Poor nutrition impacts your memory in at least three ways. First, nutrition affects your overall health. Anything short of a well-balanced diet with a large variety of good food reduces your body's vitality and ability to withstand stress. Good eating habits prevent assaults on memory caused by nutrition deficiencies and provide you with added reserves for coping with other memory stressors, such as illness or medications.

A second way nutrition affects memory is through its impact on the circulatory system. Diets high in saturated fat contribute to cholesterol build-up in the blood and fatty deposits on artery walls. Such circulatory problems increase blood pressure and can reduce oxygen flow to the brain. A diet low in fats gives added memory protection.

The third way nutrition interacts with memory is through vitamins and minerals. The brain needs a vast array of vitamins, minerals and trace elements to work at its best. Deficiencies in any needed substances can alter brain chemistry and impair the memory. Deficiencies in thiamine, vitamin B-12, vitamin B-6, and folate deficiencies have been linked to memory loss and mental impairment.

Research continues to identify the specific vitamins and minerals needed as protection against mental decline. The research is complex and long-term. Until more answers are known, the best course of action is to maintain a well-balanced diet with an ample variety of fresh foods. One more hint: because dehydration can also bring on memory loss, drinking a glass of water several times a day is a good, low-cost way to further protect your memory. (People diagnosed as having congestive heart failure should talk with their doctor before increasing the amount of water they drink.)

Inactivity

Exercise which raises your pulse and requires you to breathe more deeply over a period of ten minutes or longer tends to expand and protect your body's ability to deliver oxygen to the brain. Lack of physical activity can be a contributing factor in memory loss.

Infections

Infections, particularly in older adults, can cause sudden impairments to memory. While a bad cold or the flu can noticeably weaken memory, more severe infections such as encephalitis, tuberculosis or abscesses can produce the full signs of dementia. Memory is usually restored when the infection is treated.

Heart and lung disease

Cardiovascular and pulmonary illnesses are often accompanied by memory problems due to these diseases' effects on the blood supply to the brain. If untreated, the effects can be permanent.

Thyroid problems and other diseases

Older persons under treatment for thyroid problems may also experience changes in memory acuity. Liver failure, kidney failure, glucose abnormalities and pituitary problems also raise the risks of memory impairment.

Alcohol

Everyone knows that if you drink too much at a party, you won't remember much about it the next day. It is also true that even a few drinks can impair your memory of what is happening while you are drinking. The long-term effects of alcohol on memory are also significant. The amount of alcohol drunk **per occasion** has a greater effect on memory than does the **total** consumption. Having a glass of wine every evening would have far less long-term impact on memory than would drinking seven glasses once a week.

Alcoholism can have a devastating and sometimes irreversible effect on memory. Alcohol affects different people in different ways. It is impossible to accurately predict at what point memory problems become severe. Drinking no more than two drinks a day, or perhaps less than that if memory loss concerns you, is a good guide.

Limited sight and hearing

Memory problems are also caused by poor sight and hearing. When the initial sensory message is blurred or garbled, the poor learning which follows will often be thought to be a memory problem. When the message is not clear, the brain does not find it interesting enough to save. For example, the hearing impaired person who tires of asking others to speak more clearly will often just tune out and register nothing in his or her memory.

The hearing or vision loss may be permanent, but you can compensate for the loss through eyeglasses, good lighting, magnifiers, hearing aids and environments with few distractions.

Irreversible memory loss

Irreversible memory loss occurs when injury or disease damages the brain. Traumatic injury to the head and cerebral strokes cause large numbers of memory cells to die. When this occurs there is no way to revive the lost memory. Other conditions such as Alzheimer's disease and some other dementing illnesses are also thought to produce irreversible memory loss. Because these illnesses seem to disrupt the retrieval process rather than permanently destroy memory cells, future research and breakthroughs in self-treatment methods may someday make memory restoration possible.

> *It isn't so astonishing the number of things I can remember as the number of things I remember that aren't so.*
>
> *Mark Twain*

Common memory complaints

Despite the fact that memory skills decline very little with normal aging, complaints about forgetfulness are widespread among older adults. Almost universally, older people are concerned about memory. Forgetting names, appointments or whether the door is locked become common annoyances which can start concerns about mental status. In most cases, these concerns and complaints are overstated in comparison to how well the memory actually works.

The cause of such a high level of complaints can be linked to at least three things. First, the need for more time and more memory cues to retrieve information is noticeable and annoying. Forgetting names is particularly frustrating because you often have only a few seconds to respond. As the older person accepts the idea that his or her memory has to work harder now to find information, complaints about the problem subside.

A second cause of memory complaints relates directly to the reversible causes of memory loss discussed earlier. Depression, for example, does lower memory performance—but not half as much as it increases memory complaints. The depressed person who forgets where he put his keys will often assume that his memory is completely gone. Depressed people who perform well on memory tests still complain more about their memories than nondepressed people who have memory impairment.

The third cause of memory complaints is linked to expectations that memory loss and senility are a part of old age. People who have been forgetting names and faces all of their lives with no real concern suddenly become alarmed by their forgetfulness when they reach 65. Because of their negative expectations, they think each forgotten item is an early sign of dementia. Once a person develops positive expectations about staying mentally alert throughout life, complaints about memory loss become less significant.

Common memory complaints

The following are common responses made by older adults to the question "What does it annoy you to forget?"

- *Names*

- *Where I've put things*

- *What I've read*

- *Important tasks or appointments*

- *What I want to say*

- *Dates (bill paying)*

- *Names of movies and books*

- *Numbers*

- *To take along the things I need*

- *Medicine*

- *Who I've called on the phone.*

Memory enhancement

Regardless of how well your memory works, you can train it to work better. People of any age can learn memory skills which will help them remember more and retrieve things more quickly.

Memory protection

The first step toward improving your memory is to learn to protect your memory. By protecting your memory, you prevent the many common causes of memory loss from affecting you. Six specific things you can do to protect your memory are:

1. **Eat well.**
   A good balanced diet, high in fruits, vegetables, calcium and protein and low in fats and sugars will help avoid memory-reducing illness.

2. **Exercise.**
   Regular exercise will increase circulation and raise your spirits. Both contribute to good memory.

3. **Minimize medications.**
   Work with your physician and pharmacist to reduce the dosages of medications to the minimum effective level. Eliminate, if possible, the memory-limiting drugs described on page 58.

4. **Limit your alcohol.**
Two or more drinks per day on a routine basis can impair your memory. Try limiting how much you drink.

5. **Laugh and smile.**
Depression is one of the biggest causes of memory loss. Stay happy and you will have more to remember.

6. **Use it or lose it.**
The more you use your memory, the longer it will last.

Memory training

Older adults are often able to improve their scores on memory tests twenty to thirty percent by participating in memory training. Memory training often involves improved attention, visual imagery and grouping.

Improved attention

Attention determines what gets into your primary or short-term memory. Where you place your attention will decide what you learn and how well you remember it. Older people often have difficulty dividing their attention between two or more activities. The use of relaxation techniques such as the progressive muscle relaxation exercise described on page 67 has been shown to improve memory performance. Other focusing

techniques such as the Name/Face Remembering technique on page 44 can greatly improve memory skills and speed.

Visual imagery

Creating a visual image of a name or thing has been shown to be a highly effective memory aid. Techniques such as the Name-Face Visualization method presented on page 46 use mental pictures to provide additional cues for remembering.

Grouping

As described on page 51, grouping is a simple memory training technique which recognizes that several small lists of related items are easier to remember than one long list of unrelated items.

Memory aids

When a person uses a calendar, notepad or other memory aid to avoid forgetting things, it is not a sign of a bad memory; it is a sign of good management. No matter how good your memory, memory aids can help you be more efficient. Why clutter your mind with details which are easily recorded elsewhere?

Calendars

Perhaps the best all-around memory aid ever designed is the appointment calendar. You can record important times, dates and places you wish to remember. Use your calendar for everything you need to recall. If you need to go out for a few errands on Tuesday, write them on your calendar and take it with you. Once you get in the habit of using it you will be able to avoid the inconvenience of the missed appointment or forgotten errand. When carried with you all the time, a calendar can become a helpful planning guide, recording all commitments, appointments and opportunities to have a good time.

Daily reminders

Your calendar can aid your memory in a million ways. Use it to remember:

- *Your anniversary*

- *Lunch*

- *A visit with ET*

- *What to take to the picnic*

- *Dinner with Andre'*

- *Time for a check-up*

- *Time to get a new calendar*

- *Hot dates of all types*

- *Grandchildren's birthdays*

- *Dinner with your daughter*

- *Where the hike begins*

- *Time for a tune-up*

- *Time for a pull-up*

- *Arbor Day*

and on and on and on...

Notepads

In addition to a calendar, it is handy to always have a notepad with you and to use it to write down anything of importance. Write down the names of the people you meet (if you want to remember them), the grocery list, your doctor's recommendations, or the idea you have for a senior center fund-raising project. Business people almost always write letters, memos, or minutes to record important information. A well-used notepad can help you do the same.

Chalkboard

Another useful memory device is a chalkboard or bulletin board near your telephone. Get in the habit of leaving notes for yourself or others and check it every time you enter or leave the house.

Other memory aids

In addition to the all-purpose memory aids described there are many aids helpful to remember specific things. A few examples are:

Alarm wrist watch -
to remind you when it is time to go.

Eyeglass keeper -
a cord that goes around your neck so you don't lose your glasses when you put them down.

Special place for keys -
get into the habit of putting your keys in a bowl by the door every time you come home. You will always be able to find them when you leave.

Cooking timer -
always set it and never turn it off until you have turned off the oven and burners.

Bill collector -
keep all your bills to be paid in a single envelope or box. As they are paid, write "paid" on them and file them away.

Medical insurance notebook -
keep a separate notebook for medical insurance with columns for your doctor's name, date of service, the amount to be paid and insurance and Medicare reimbursement.

Address book -
for keeping names, addresses, phone numbers and birthdates for as many people as you wish. Add your address book to your calendar and carry the combined book with you.

Medication box -
a box with compartments for the medicines you need to take at each time of the day. If you take medicines twice a day, a medication box with fourteen compartments would work for a whole week. Fill it on Sunday with all the right pills. You will always be able to tell whether you have already taken the pill. See page 66.

Positive attitudes and memory

If you like yourself and look forward to a positive future, your overall memory will improve. Study after study shows memory performance can be improved as much through enhancement of self-image as through memory training. Perhaps it is no more than having good things to remember, but those who feel good inside can retrieve information faster and more accurately.

The best way to expand your memory is to be nice to yourself. Spend more time with people who make you feel good. Do the things that help you reach your goals. When your life is on track and you are positive about the future, your memory will work for you.

The sage looks at memory

The next time you find yourself complaining about your memory, make an appointment to discuss it with the sage within you. Chances are that your sage, using the *Growing Wiser* Formula, plus some good common sense, will help you improve both your memory and your appreciation of it.

Your sage might first help you recognize how well your memory really works. Put in perspective, your forgetfulness is probably only a bother and poses no significant problem to your life.

Next, your sage might suggest that you turn to him or her more often. The sage knows that wisdom is a higher form of memory. By raising your expectations about memory, the sage within will release much more of your concern about memory and actually help you remember more.

Finally, your sage may talk you into trying the memory aids above or the memory training activities on the following pages. Remembering is one of the most beautiful things of life. By listening to your sage, you will remember more and better appreciate your memory.

Memory is the treasury and guardian of all things.
Cicero

Recommended Reading

Memory by Elizabeth Loftus. Reading, MA: Addison-Wesley, 1982.

The Memory Book by Harry Lorayne and Jerry Lucas. New York: Ballantine Books, 1974.

Growing Younger by Donald W. Kemper, Judith Deneen and Jim Giuffre'. Boise: Healthwise, Inc., 1982.

A Little Mixed Up

Just a line to say I'm living
   That I'm not among the dead.
Though I'm getting more forgetful
   And more "mixed up" in the head.

For sometimes I can't remember
   When I stand at foot of stairs,
If I must go up for something
   Or if I've just come down from
   there.

And before the refrigerator so often
   My poor mind is filled with doubt.
Have I just put food away or
   Have I come to take something
   out?

And there's times when it is dark out
   With my night cap on my head
I don't know if I'm retiring
   Or just getting out of bed.

So if it's my turn to write you
   There's no need getting sore.
I may think I've written
   And don't want to be a bore.

So remember I do love you
   And wish you were here.
But now it is nearly meal time
   So I'm saying "Good bye, dear."

There I stood beside the mailbox
   With my face so very red.
Instead of mailing my letter
   I opened it instead.

        Alton E. Smith

Memory Shift

Just a call to say I'm living
   That I'm active and well fed
Though I'm occasionally forgetful
   When something else is in my head.

Like the times I can't remember
   When I meet you on the stairs
Just what name to call you
   Though I truly know it's there.

You see my mind is active
   Filled with wonder and unrest
And names don't always surface
   At the time it would be best.

So when you think my mind's a blank
   Or that my brain has gone away
I may be only thinking of how
   The world is new today.

My memory's been changing
   As I've grown upon the earth
I've lost some of the crispness
   Of recall - but not the worth.

Instead of lightning speed
   For citing faces, names and places,
I tend to think things through
   And try to find new clues and
   traces.

My memory has lots to store
   And acts much as a miser
It works on what's important first...
   That's part of *Growing Wiser*.

        D.K.

Name/Face Remembering

I used to have trouble remembering names
until I took that Sam Carnegie course.
Jack Taylor

People complain about forgetting names more than any other memory problem. It is of particular concern because some people feel embarrassed when they cannot recall the name of the person when they meet.

For names you would like to remember, there are two basic ways to improve your memory:

1. Learn the names better

2. Develop a memory cue which links the name to the person

This activity will help you improve how well you learn peoples' names and how quickly you can remember them the next time you meet.

Learning names better

Most of the names you cannot remember are not forgotten—they were never fully learned in the first place. The next time you are introduced to a new person STOP, LOOK AND LISTEN!

1. **STOP!**
   Before you reach out to shake hands with a new person, stop and think, **"STOP, I want to remember this person."** Stopping means concentrating on the person in front of you and clearing your mind of other distractions. Use the handshake as a cue to stop and focus on learning the person's name.

2. **LOOK!**
   Look at the person's face while you talk to him or her. Say to yourself, **"Look at this interesting face."** Also look at the person's name tag if he or she has one.

3. **LISTEN!**
   Concentrate on hearing the name of the person clearly. Say to yourself **"Listen to this person's name."** If you are not sure you heard the name correctly, repeat what you thought you heard and ask if that is correct. Don't rush to the next person—keep shaking the hand until you have heard the name clearly and repeated it correctly.

4. **WRITE!**
   If you have the chance, write the name down as soon as you can and study it a few minutes later. The visual reinforcement will help you remember the names even better.

The Stop, Look and Listen advice alone will more than double your ability to remember new names. The introductions may take a few minutes longer, but the names will be much easier to remember.

> *Remember:*
> *STOP, I want to remember this person.*
> *LOOK, this is an interesting face.*
> *LISTEN to this person's name.*

Names and Faces: Remembering Names With Visualization

Memory and the senses

Everything you learn comes through your senses—primarily through what you see and what you hear, but also through what you touch, smell or taste. Remembering, too, involves the senses. In remembering names and faces, you must link the visual memory of the person's face with the sound of his/her name.

The stronger the image you have of the name and the person, the more easily you will be able to remember the name in the future.

One of the best memory training methods ever devised is the use of visual images to link names and faces. The method is fairly simple, but it takes a little imagination and some practice. It fits in well with the STOP, LOOK and LISTEN method.

Step 1. **STOP—**
As you clear your mind to remember this person, get ready to visualize.

Step 2. **LOOK—**
As you look at the person, search for a distinctive feature on his/her face: a high forehead, a beautiful smile, a big nose, a mole, anything.

Step 3. **LISTEN—**
As you hear the name, try to associate it with something you can visualize. For example, if the name is Molly Mettler, you might associate "Mettler" with something made of metal; or the name "Matzek" with a door mat slashed with the mark of Zorro. Your image for "Kemper" could be someone losing his temper.

Step 4. **LINK—**
The final step is to link the visual image of the name with the prominent feature on the person's face. For example:

If Molly Mettler has a distinctive smile or mouth, imagine that the mouth was made of metal. Molly Metalmouth will from then on be unforgettable.

If Betty Matzek has curly hair, imagine that it is really a doormat with a Z slashed across it. You would always think Betty Mat-z when you see her.

If Don Kemper has a ruddy complexion, imagine him turning brighter red from his temper. Don Temper would come to mind when he enters the room.

If Jim Giuffre' (Jufray) has a raggedy moustache, imagine that he chews on it causing it to become frayed. Thus, he would be remembered as Jim Chew-fray.

Now you might think that this could get very embarrassing. Suppose you slipped up and actually called Molly Mettler by the name Miss Metalmouth? Don't worry, it is not likely to happen. Your memory only needs some cues with which to "look" for the name. Metalmouth is a great cue to help your brain pull out the right name.

Learning the method

1. Practice looking for distinctive features. Open the newspaper and look at all the close-up pictures of people. Next turn to the editorial page and notice how cartoonists always exaggerate one feature of each famous person they draw.

2. Practice developing a visual image for a name. Decide on one or more visual images for each of the following names.

    a. Roger Fuller   e. Lee Gray
    b. Pat Gardner   f. Barbara Grigg
    c. Ted Gorosin   g. Joe Gwartney
    d. Opal Givens   h. Marcus Hall

    Examples:

    a. Roger Fuller with square shoulders could have an overflowing (full) pitcher of water on each shoulder.

b. Pat Gardner with bushy eyebrows could have a small gardener tending a garden in her eyebrows.

c. Ted Gorosin with a balding head could have a small garrison circling his bald spot.

d. Opal Givens with a pointed nose could have a white flag on top of it saying "I give in."

You can use the telephone book to get more names for additional practice.

3. Practice linking the visual image and the distinctive feature. Do it for the people whose closeups are in the newspaper.

This visualization method takes some practice to master. But just trying it along with the STOP, LOOK and LISTEN method will help you immensely.

The Graceful Cover-up

I always depend on the kindness of strangers.
Blanche DuBois
from "A Streetcar Named Desire"

Imagine yourself at the grocery store when across the banana display you see a person with whom you used to work. You know that person's name like your own—but it just doesn't come to mind. What should you do?

   A.   Pretend you don't see the person and walk away?
   B.   Turn yourself in for immediate mental evaluation?
   C.   Tell your old friend that your mind is on bananas right now and his name must have slipped out on one of the peels?

The graceful cover-up is a way to slip out of forgetfulness situations without embarrassing or insulting either yourself or the other person. Clearly option A., the pretend-not-to-see-and-walk-out option, is insulting to the other person; option B., is selling yourself short. What you need is a way to break through the awkwardness with something witty or humorous which leaves both you and the other person feeling good.

Exercise: For each of the following situations, develop a graceful cover-up which will help you through the situation:

Situation #1
You are sitting with your best friend at a restaurant when an old friend walks over and says hello. You want to introduce your old friend to your best friend, but you can't think of her name. GRACEFUL COVER-UP:

Situation #1: To your best friend: "Bob, I'd like you to meet one of my old friends from back in the days when my memory was concerned with names," - or "but my memory is playing hide and seek again."

Situation #2

You were introduced to a person at a party and spent the next five minutes finding out you have much in common. As you start to leave, you realize that you have completely forgotten his name. GRACEFUL COVER-UP:

Situation #2: "You are such an interesting person that I don't want to forget your name. Could you tell me again so that I can write it down?"

Situation #3

You have been asked to present the Outstanding Club Member of the Year award to a person you have worked with for the past 10 years. As you begin your remarks, you realize that you can't think of her name. GRACEFUL COVER-UP: (Fainting is not acceptable!)

Situation #3: **Excuse yourself for a moment while you ask the person for her full** name. Then start over.

Grouping of Lists

Any list of items is easier to remember if you can group them into categories. For example, suppose you wished to remember to buy the following items at the grocery store:

1. apples
2. toilet paper
3. bread
4. pickles
5. Newsweek
6. milk

7. bananas
8. calcium pills
9. potatoes
10. tea
11. cereal

12. orange juice
13. light bulbs
14. lettuce
15. peanut butter
16. carrots

With very little effort, you could list the items by group as indicated below (of course a written list would be even better).

Fresh fruit & vegetable group	Other food	Drinks	Non-food
apples	bread	milk	toilet paper
bananas	pickles	tea	Newsweek
potatoes	cereal	orange juice	calcium pills
lettuce	peanut butter		light bulbs
carrots			

Remedies For Forgetfulness

1. List below the four things you are most likely to forget (example: names, keys, purse, to lock the door, etc.):

   a. _____

   b. _____

   c. _____

   d. _____

2. For each one, review pages 39-41 to consider how memory aids can help you in the future. Discuss with others how they would remember each **thing** on your list. Write your action plan below:

   ACTION PLAN - To stop forgetting

   a. _____

   _____

   b. _____

   _____

   c. _____

   _____

   d. _____

   _____

Chapter 3

Mental Alertness

He who lives by his wits, dies with his wits.

David Krech

One of the most persistent myths of aging is that mental decline is inevitable. The doddering, confused senior citizen is an image constantly evoked by the media, our youth-oriented society and often older people themselves. For many, this image begins a lifelong concern that the mind, as well as the body, will increasingly show signs of age.

As with the physical body, the passing of time does bring biological changes to the brain. There is a reduction of speed in the retrieval of facts from the memory and a slowing down of assimilation of new information. In tests that measure intelligence, older people have tended to sacrifice speed in favor of accuracy... not such a bad idea, all things considered.

"The human brain does not shrink, wilt, perish or deteriorate with age."

Dr. Alex Comfort in his book **A Good Age** goes on to state, "...several studies show that there is virtually no sign of decline in the intelligence of normal, healthy individuals past sixty."

> *Reject the myth that learning is for young people. It is what you learn after you know it all that counts.*
> *John Gardener*

Keeping your marbles: Preventing dementia

Senility. Losing your marbles. Dementia. These are words which raise red flags of alarm for many people. In truth, loss of mental capacity in old age is uncommon. Losing your marbles is statistically an unlikely occurrence. By conservative estimates, less than 10 percent of all people over 65 will, to any degree, become "demented;" nine out of ten older adults retain mental vitality throughout their lives.

A number of conditions that **mimic** mental deterioration do exist. The consequences of poor diet, alcohol, overuse of medications, infection, disease, depression and social isolation (to name just a few) produce symptoms of mental confusion. When this happens, it is called a pseudo-dementia or false dementia.

If detected and managed, these conditions are reversible. However, it is a far better thing to prevent them from occurring in the first place. At any age, self-care is an important part of retaining optimal functioning of mind and body. With proper care you can maintain and even improve your mental vitality as long as you live.

About Alzheimer's disease

Unless you have recently returned from an extended solo backpack trip through Nepal, you have probably seen articles and stories in the popular press about Alzheimer's disease. Alzheimer's disease is a disorder of the cells of the brain which causes progressive damage to brain tissue. There is no known way to reverse or cure it.

Touted as the "Disease of the Century," Alzheimer's has had extensive media coverage in recent years. While informative and enlightening, this media exposure has created a climate of alarm about Alzheimer's which is significantly out of proportion to the disease's occurrence in the population.

Alzheimer's disease, or any other kind of dementia, is not a normal part of aging. Only five percent of people in their sixties are possibly affected by Alzheimer's. The incidence increases with each decade of age.

A check-up from the neck-up

Do you ever wonder if you are losing your mind? You may be noticing that you forget things, or can't remember names, or feel confused at times and wonder if these are early signs of dementia. A check-up from the neck-up is an easy way to tell whether there is any real cause for concern. Try this three-step procedure:

**Step one:
Identify the clues**

Have you or anyone you know had any major and lasting changes in any or all of the following areas:

- **Personality—**
  for example, when a normally social person becomes very withdrawn or when he or she often responds inappropriately to a situation or if wild mood swings are apparent.

- **Behavior—**
  for example, when a normally tidy person no longer pays attention to personal grooming or when an easy-going person becomes aggressive.

- **Skills—**
  for example, when a person, once able to balance a checkbook, finds it extremely difficult to do simple calculations, or if any simple, well-known task, such as putting on

makeup or brewing a cup of tea, becomes hard to do.

- **Orientation—**
  for example, when a person gets confused or lost on roads which were once very familiar.

If the occurrences are minor or infrequent, these changes are more likely to be causes for frustration than alarm.

A Rule of Thumb

If you go to a store and forget what you came to buy, it's of little mental concern—next time bring a list. If you forget what you are supposed to do in the store—that's serious.

Step two:
Identify the reason

Is there a reason which might explain the change? A very depressed person or a person who is grieving over the loss of a loved one may show some of the changes mentioned in Step One.

If there is no readily identifiable reason for the changes and if they happen frequently, you might request a "geriatric assessment" from qualified professionals.

Step three:
Check it out

You need to find out whether the problem is serious, what the cause is, and what might be done to reverse it. First, try a do-it-yourself assessment and then share it with your physician. This will help you determine if a more detailed assessment would be appropriate. If there is a problem, a detailed assessment can find the root cause of the problem and start changes which restore both joy and productivity to living. The assessment could be performed by a "geriatric assessment team." This team can include a physician, nurse, psychologist, social worker and others with special training in diagnosing the problems of older adults. Note – most physicians receive little training in the mental assessment of older people. Because your doctor may know you well, he or she should review your concerns before referring you to a geriatric specialist or assessment team.

	Self-assessment	**Professional Assessment**
How serious?	Review Step One and determine if the changes are causing problems in daily living.	The assessment team will interview the individual and those close to him to build a behavior profile of the individual.
Cause?	Ask if any of the following could be a problem: Depression (see pg. 60) Poor nutrition Stress Medications (see pg. 58) Illness Alcohol	The team will do a full physical exam to study virtually all possible causes. Medical histories, dietary analysis, and psychological examinations are often done to identify the real problem.
What to do about it	Think positive and follow the guidelines in Chapters 2 and 3.	The team will recommend changes in your medications, diet, or other activities which you may find helpful.

Medicine management

Medicines can have a great deal of impact upon your mental alertness. Drugs are powerful substances. When used wisely, they play an important role in maintaining good health. Taking medication in doses or combinations that have a negative effect on your physical and mental health is known as *drug intoxication*. This can happen with both over-the-counter drugs, such as cough syrup and decongestants, and those you get through prescriptions.

Research shows that medicines stay in the body longer in older people. What may be a safe dose at age 45 can be an overdose at age 70. Often, older people could use a smaller dosage than is regularly prescribed.

Check through the following list of drugs which are known to negatively affect memory and mental alertness. If you are taking any of these and feel they may be affecting your mental alertness, discuss it with your physician or pharmacist. He or she may be able to suggest changes in your treatment plan which could pose less risk to your mental alertness.

Drugs which can have a negative effect on memory and mental alertness (*Important)

1. *Drugs which act on the brain*

- *Major tranquilizers*, e.g., chlorpromazine, haloperidol*
- *Minor tranquilizers*, e.g., diazepam, chlordiazepoxide*
- *Sleeping tablets (hypnotics)*, e.g., lorazepam*
- *Parkinson drugs, e.g., levodopa*
- *Anti-histamine drugs, e.g., promethazine*
- *Anti-depressants, e.g., amitriptyline, imipramine*

2. *Some blood pressure drugs* (Many do not affect memory or alertness so alternatives can be selected.)*

- *reserpine, clonidine, methyldopa*
- *propranolol*

3. *Pain-killers*

- *e.g., non steriodal - ibuprofen, naproxen*
- *e.g., codeine, etc.*
- *Note: acetaminophen (Tylenol) does not affect memory or mental alertness*

4. *Anti-cholinergic drugs* (Stomach relaxers)*

- *Broad range of drugs including many of the above.*

Action plans for managing medications

You are the person best qualified to keep yourself healthy. As a consumer, it is up to you to work in partnership with doctors, pharmacists and other health care providers for a health regimen that works for you.

Five things you can do to ensure the best medicine management for yourself are:

1. Give and receive clear information when you visit your doctor or doctors. If you see more than one doctor, be sure to tell him or her what drugs your other physicians have prescribed for you.

   • Prepare a written list of things to tell the doctor and include questions you want to ask. Be sure to ask about any possible drug effects on your mental alertness.

   • Bring all the medicines you are using, including non-prescription drugs.

   • Bring a written list of your allergies or the drugs to which you have a negative reaction.

2. Avoid or limit medications when possible.

   • Ask your doctor to discuss any alternatives to medication, such as exercise or diet.

   • Be particularly concerned about the drugs listed on page 58.

3. Get complete information about medicine from your doctor or pharmacist.

   • If you have trouble with child-proof caps on your medicines, ask for easy-to-open caps.

   • Ask how to save money by using generic drugs.

4. Organize a system for taking your medicines.

   • Turn to page 66 in this handbook for some systems to help you organize your medications.

5. Know what to do when a medicine causes negative side effects.

   • When a medicine is prescribed, ask the doctor how you should expect to feel and what to do if other symptoms develop.

   • Take medicines as directed.

Pick and choose from these suggestions. Not every idea will be right for everyone. You will know which tool is best for you.

Depression

Depression is a potent mental de-vitalizer. Depression can rob you of your memory, your alertness and your pizazz. Depression is wide-spread; it has been called "the common cold of mental disorders." Call it what you will, the blahs or the blues, chances are there has been a time when you felt your life did not hold its usual gusto and promise.

Everyone goes through occasional bouts with the blues. Sadness, grief and discouragement are part of life. However, depression is different from sadness or grief, both of which can be a healthy reaction to loss, disappointment or misfortune. Depression is when you feel stuck in your sad, bad feelings and when these feelings interfere with daily life.

The symptoms of depression

Some of the symptoms of depression have a lot in common with the feelings you might have on a cold, rainy Monday: anxiety, irritability, loss of energy and difficulty in concentrating and making decisions. If you notice a significant change (increase or decrease) in your eating and sleeping patterns, if you feel like crying all the time, or if you are pre-occupied by thoughts about death and suicide, the blues may have taken hold.

What causes depression?

Depression may be triggered by a significant change or loss in your life: the death of a loved one, sickness, a personal hurt or misfortune. Other elements which may lead to the blues include poor nutrition, unrelieved stress, allergies, hormonal imbalance, medication reactions, difficulty in expressing anger, frustration at work or home, changes of season or even holidays like Christmas.

Self-care for the blues

While severe depression often requires professional treatment, there is a lot you can do to help get through the blues. If you are feeling low, try the following activities:

- Recognize that you are coming down with something. Treat yourself gently and lovingly, and that includes your body.

- Keep on going on. It is easier to **do** yourself into **feeling** better than to **feel** yourself into **doing** better.

- Try exercise. Several studies show that regular, vigorous exercise such as walking, swimming or bicycling not only relieves stress but elevates moods as well.

- Get by with a little help from your friends. Talk with them about your blues. Support from friends and family can be a godsend when you are down.

• Manage your medicine before it manages you. Sleeping pills, tranquilizers, some blood pressure medications, "water pills," some stomach medications and a host of other medications may be causing your blues. Check with your doctor if you think your medications are causing you to feel down.

• Go in search of a belly laugh. Look for it everywhere, in books, movies, cartoons or your eccentric next-door neighbor. Laughter and the blues just don't go together.

• Change distorted and irrational thinking! Become aware of any negative messages you are giving yourself through self-talk, the internal dialogue that goes on constantly in your mind.

Irrational thinking: What you think is what you get

A useful self-care tool for the treatment and relief of depression is cognitive therapy—changing the way you think. This approach, developed by Aaron Beck, M.D., of the University of Pennsylvania School of Medicine, suggests that distorted, irrational and negative thinking leads to negative emotions. In other words: your thoughts create your feelings. If your thoughts and messages to yourself shout "defeated, defective,

deserted and deprived!"—well, who wouldn't feel a little down at the mouth?

Twelve types of negative thinking

• **All or nothing thinking—** thinking you have to be perfect to be worthwhile:
"I'm never going to be five-foot two with eyes of blue—I'm a total failure."

• **Overgeneralization—** concluding that a negative event will happen time and time again:
"I am always waited upon by rude salespeople—they're out to get me."

• **Under-rating and disqualifying the positive—** insisting that positive experiences don't count and changing them into negative events:
"Out of 344 members, 343 voted to elect me as club president. That one person must be right."

• **Mental filter—** dwelling exclusively on a single negative detail:
"I stepped on my partner's toes while doing the tango. The whole evening was ruined."

• **Jumping to conclusions—** jumping to a negative conclusion that is not justified by the facts:
"Thelma didn't say hello today.

She must think I'm getting senile. I guess she's right."

- **Fortune telling—**
anticipating the worst and convincing yourself that this is fact:
    "I'm going to make an utter fool of myself at the church social. I'd better stay home."

- **Mind reading —**
concluding that someone is reacting negatively to you without checking out the facts:
    "Bob doesn't stop by for coffee anymore. He thinks I'm boring."

- **Magnification or minimization—**
amplifying your faults and discounting your successes:
    "I can't waltz and will never learn to waltz and I'm a terrible dancer even if I did place first in the jitterbug contest."

- **Emotional reasoning—**
"I feel it, therefore, it must be true." Assuming that your negative emotions reflect the way things really are:
    "I feel discouraged and hopeless. Therefore, my problems are impossible to solve."

- **Should statements—**
using "should," "ought" and "must" to motivate yourself, thereby paving the way to guilt and self-blame:
    "I shouldn't be angry with Jean even though this is the sixth

time she's let me down."

- **Labeling—**
attaching a label to yourself, or others, instead of describing the error:
    "I burnt dinner. I'm stupid and incompetent."

- **Personalization—**
assuming responsibility for a negative event you did not cause:
    "The rummage sale didn't make as much money as we hoped. It's my fault."

Do any of these irrational statements sound familiar? If so, you may want to begin beating the blues and bolstering your self-esteem by getting the best of your negative self-talk.

> *Be not afraid of life. Believe that life is worth living, and your belief will help create the fact.*
> *William James*

Neutralizing your nay-sayer

Most importantly, talk back to your internal critic. Would you stand by passively while someone said terrible things about someone you love? Probably not. Put your internal critic in his rightful place.

Dr. David Burns, in his book **Feeling Good: The New Mood Therapy,** suggests a three-step process to combatting negative thinking and raising your self-esteem:

- Write down your negative thoughts. This helps train you to recognize self-critical messages as they go through your mind.

- Compare these statements to the twelve types of negative thinking listed earlier and see which apply to your negative self-talk.

- Put things in perspective and develop a more realistic way of evaluating yourself.

Write down your thoughts. Get them out of your head and onto paper. Step back and take the long view. With practice, you can learn to replace the negative messages that lead to lowered self-esteem and depression with a more realistic and positive outlook.

> *You've got to accentuate the positive,*
> *Eliminate the negative,*
> *Latch onto the affirmative,*
> *Don't mess with Mr. In-between.*
> *from a song by Johnny Mercer*

Relaxation

Accentuating the positive and eliminating the negative is a lot easier if your body is physically calm and relaxed. Tranquil thoughts and up-beat mental images require a tension-free body to do their work.

The body responds to tense thoughts or situations with muscle tension which, in turn, causes pain and discomfort. Muscle relaxation and simple breathing techniques are a great help in reducing tension and relieving stress. A deep muscle relaxation exercise designed to help soothe body and soul can be found on page 67.

Breathing exercises such as roll breathing (see page 70) and the relaxing sigh (page 71) will reduce stress and oxygenate your brain for clearer and more positive thinking.

Best of all, a technique that will relax both you and someone else: the shoulder and neck massage. See page 72 for instructions.

Beyond self-care

At what point should you seek professional help for the treatment of depression? We can all expect to have blue periods resulting from life's ups and downs, and usually, time heals all wounds. However, if even after trying some of the self-care tips on page 60, your period of despondency seems to be dragging on and if your distress interferes with your daily activities, it is appropriate to explore an additional course of treatment. (By all means, continue with the self-care options; they'll do no harm and probably a world of good.)

Work in cooperation with a health care professional to rule out physical causes first, such as drug intoxication, hormonal imbalance or nutritional inadequacies, to name a few. If there is no physical basis for your depression, find a therapist, (for example, a psychiatrist, psychologist, or psychiatric social worker) skilled in the treatment of mood disorders. Experienced friends, your health care provider, your pastor or the local mental health association can help you in locating a suitable therapist.

An up note about feeling down

Even though many older people, like people of all ages, suffer from depression, try not to take it lying down. Depression is not a natural part of aging. It can be treated with self-care techniques and, if necessary, professional help.

It is no fun being down in the dumps, but depression, like any other pain or illness, can provide a valuable opportunity for self-evaluation and growth. It serves as an indicator that something within you needs attention and change. And sometimes, emerging successfully and whole from a period of despondency can bring deeper meaning and appreciation to your life.

The sage and lifelong mental vitality

The care and feeding of your mind is a lifetime commitment. Protect the sage within you and your mental resources by taking care of your body —eating the right foods, watching your medications, relaxing and getting enough oxygen through steady exercise. It means paying attention to your emotional state—pulling yourself out of depression, loving and forgiving yourself, seeking out the support and friendship of others and going in search of things that bring you pleasure.

The trick to developing mental muscle and making the most of your mental vitality is to use it! Stimulation is the key. Sitting home all day, glued to the television set, will not exercise your mind. Memory and all other mental activity can be improved through lifelong learning and care. Your mind requires change, input and enrichment. It is up to you to nurture, stretch and flex your mind into mental wellness.

The mind is like a parachute - it only functions when open.
Jack Goldstein

Recommended Reading

Feeling Good: The New Mood Therapy by David Burns. New York: William Morrow and Company, 1980.

Your Second Life by Gay Gaer Luce. New York: Delacorte Press, 1979.

Growing Older, Growing Better by Jane Porcino. Reading, MA: Addison Wesley, 1983.

The Lively Mind by Jules Z. Willing. New York: Quill, 1982.

Medication Systems*

If you take the same medicines in the same dosages every day, a daily container system might be helpful. The daily container works best if you only take a few pills per day and if it is easy to tell the difference (in shapes and colors) between them. The daily container can be a cup. Every morning you put the medicines you will be taking that day in a cup. At any time during the day, you can then determine how many pills you have taken up to that point by counting how many are left in the cup. That way, you will never take more each day than you should.

If you take several pills several times a day—or if two of your medicines look alike—you might want to have several containers (say a morning cup and an afternoon cup). An egg container would serve the same purpose. The egg carton has 12 cups which you can label for 12 hours of the day.

Each morning, you can put the day's pills in the proper egg cups. At four in the afternoon, for example, you would take all the pills that are in the cup marked "4." If, at 4:20 in the afternoon, you cannot remember if you took your afternoon pills, just check the carton.

If some of your prescribed medicines are to be taken every other day, or in different dosages on different days, a weekly container system could be of help. Some pharmaceutical companies produce small medication holders with a different compartment for each day of the week. If you decide that this system will work for you, see your pharmacist about getting such a container.

*From **Elder-Ed**, Public Health Service/DHHS

Muscle Relaxation

Deep muscle relaxation is effective in combatting stress-related health problems and often helps people to get to sleep. You can use a pre-recorded tape to help you go through all the muscle groups or you can do it by just tensing and relaxing each muscle group.

Procedure

For best results, practice muscle relaxation at least once and preferably twice daily. Choose a place which is dimly lit and where you will be undisturbed. Pick a place which will leave your body as supported and tension-free as possible. Beds, couches, or cushions spread on the floor offer good support. Recliner chairs, large overstuffed chairs, or two chairs, one to sit on with your head resting back against the wall and the other to support your legs, are good arrangements for people who prefer to relax in a sitting position. If you find a good system, stay with it. If you continually fall asleep, change your position and/or time of day for relaxation practice.

You will find on the next pages a list of the muscle groups. Taking them in order, tense each group hard, but not to the point of cramping. Repeat any group in which you feel excessive tension. You will probably find that you have a few areas in which you experience most of your tension. These are the areas that you probably will want to repeatedly tense and relax.

Tense each muscle group for 5 to 10 seconds, then give yourself 10 to 20 seconds to continue releasing and relaxing. At various points you should go back over and review the various muscle groups and let each go a little more, e.g., after your arms, after your neck and head area, after your chest and stomach area, and after your legs are finished. Arouse yourself thoroughly by counting backwards from five to one.

You should not practice for more than about 25 minutes at a time. This should give you time enough to tense and release each muscle group once and repeat two or three times those special muscle groups in which you experience the most tension.

Muscle groups and exercises

1. Hands by clenching them (then let them relax).

2. Wrists and forearms by extending them and bending the hands back at the wrists.

3. Upper arms by clenching your hands into fists and bending your arms at the elbows.

4. Shoulders by shrugging them.

   (Review the arms and shoulders area)

5. Forehead by wrinkling it into a deep frown.

6. Around the eyes and bridge of the nose by closing the eyes as tightly as possible.

7. Cheeks and jaws by grinning from ear to ear.

8. Around the mouth by pressing the lips together tightly.

9. Back of the neck by pressing the head back hard.

10. Front of the neck by touching the chin on the chest.

    (Review the neck and head area)

11. Chest by taking a deep breath and holding it, then exhaling.

12. Back by arching the back up and away from the support surfaces.

13. Stomach by sucking it in as far as possible.

    (Review the chest and stomach area)

14. Hips and buttocks by pressing the buttocks together tightly.

15. Thighs by pressing your knees together.

16. Lower legs by pointing the toes away and curling the toes downward at the same time.

(Review the area from the waist down)

With practice you will develop the skill to relax your muscles quickly and easily. Eventually you will be able to relax without the tensing part of the exercise.

Breathing

Breathing is the key to life. Full breathing is a good way to reduce tensions and to feel relaxed. Oxygen nourishes your tissues and organs and is essential to good mental and physical health. Too often people breathe in short, incomplete breaths which leave stagnant air in portions of the lungs and reduce the flow of oxygen to the blood.

Benefits of breathing (the relaxing way)

- reduces stress
- oxygenates mind and body
- purifies blood
- warms cold hands and feet

- filters and expels impurities
- enhances complexion
- nourishes vital organs

Don't hold your breath

Breath holding is a symptom of stress. Whenever you find yourself holding your breath, use it as a cue to take time out to relax.

Roll breathing

The object of roll breathing is to develop full use of your lungs. It can be practiced in any position, but is best learned lying down, with your knees bent.

1. Place your left hand on your abdomen and your right hand on your chest. Notice how your hands move as you breathe in and out.

2. Practice filling your lower lungs by breathing so that your left hand goes up and down while your right hand remains still. Always inhale through your nose and exhale through your mouth.

3. When you have filled and emptied your lower lungs 8-10 times with ease, add the second step to your breathing: inhale first into your lower lungs as before but then continue inhaling into your upper chest. As you do so, your right hand will rise and your left hand will fall a little as your stomach is drawn in.

4. As you exhale slowly through your mouth, make a quiet, whooshing sound as first your left hand and then your right hand falls. As you exhale, feel the tension leaving your body as you become more and more relaxed.

5. Practice breathing in and out in this manner for 3-5 minutes. Notice that the movement of your abdomen and chest is like the rolling motion of waves rising and falling.

Roll breathing should be practiced daily for several weeks until the roll breathing can be done almost anywhere. It provides you with an instant relaxation tool anytime you need one. **Caution:** some people get dizzy the first few times they try roll breathing. Get up slowly and with support.

The relaxing sigh

During the day you probably catch yourself sighing or yawning. This is generally a sign that you are not getting enough oxygen. Sighing and yawning are your body's way of remedying the situation. A sigh releases a bit of tension and can be used as a means of relaxing.

1. Sit or stand up straight.

2. Sigh deeply, letting out a sound of deep relief as the air rushes out of your lungs.

3. Don't think about inhaling—just let the air come in naturally.

4. Repeat this procedure 8 to 12 times whenever you feel the need for it. Experience the feeling of relaxation.

5. At the end of each out-breath, shake your hands away from your body as a symbol that you are throwing your tensions away.

Shoulder and Neck Massage

Ooooh, Aaaahh, Oooohh, Zzzz.
Massage Receiver

Have your partner sit comfortably in a chair. Stand behind her and suggest that she remove glasses, close her eyes, and think "I am relaxing."

1. Allow your hands to greet your partner by placing them warmly on her shoulders.

2. Apply gentle but firm and even pressure with your thumbs across the top of the shoulders. Work your way toward the neck and then back across to the ends of the shoulders.

3. Using both hands, massage across the top of the shoulders with a kneading motion.

4. Locate the vertebrae at the base of the neck. Place your thumbs on either side of the vertebrae and apply gentle but firm pressure away from the spine. Continue down the back. Do **not** press on the spine itself.

5. Locate indentations at the base of the skull on either side of the spine at the back of the head. Apply rotating pressure with your thumbs.

6. Stand beside your partner. Place one hand on her forehead and one hand behind her head for support. **Slowly and carefully** rotate the head first in one direction and then the other.

7. Stand behind your partner again and use three fingers to massage the jaw area. Have your partner clench her jaw. You will easily find the muscles that need to be rubbed.

8. Use fingers to gently massage the temples. Work across the forehead and back to the temples.

9. Bring your hands back to the shoulders and allow your hands to say "goodbye."

How do you feel? Sharing this exercise with someone is a warm and caring exchange. It is relaxing for both the giver and the receiver. Some of the steps (3, 5, 7 and 8) can also be used for self-massage.

*From: **A Healthy Old Age**, Stephanie FallCreek and Molly Mettler. New York: Haworth Press, 1984.*

Chapter 4

Loss and Life Change

Aging does not need to be hidden or denied, but can be understood, affirmed, and experienced as a process of growth by which the mystery of life is slowly revealed to us.
Henri Nouwen

The mystery of life is revealed by change and growth. To live is to grow and growing always involves change. Change is the only constant. It is as much a part of our lives as breathing. We change physically—from infants to adolescents to adults. We change roles—from son to suitor, from worker to retiree. Our relationships change too, as we evolve and as different needs come to the fore.

As years pass, life changes can become increasingly complex. By the time you are sixty or better, chances are you have experienced considerable growth and dealt with many transformations at home, at work, within yourself and with others. More and more, you may be forced or coaxed into letting go of what used to be and challenged to embrace the new. These change points are the crises, the decisive and critical times of life.

Crisis

Opportunity riding the dangerous wind

The Chinese ideogram, or word-picture, for the word "crisis" is composed of two different symbols: danger and opportunity. A time of crisis is a turning point for better or worse. The crisis of life change brings with it both vulnerability and an opportunity for growth.

The crisis of life change can be painful since any significant change entails a loss of some kind. Coming to terms with what once was and will never be again is life's toughest challenge. Crisis comes in many guises—through death, lessening of physical capacities, change in relationships or a deterioration of your environment. How you deal with the crisis will shape its outcome. You have at hand a natural, healing process which can help you adjust to significant change and loss: grief.

Good grief

Grief is good. It helps to make sense of changes, provides a period of adjustment and lays the foundation for a future which may be better and more meaningful than the past. Grieving is also a process, a series of emotions and feelings which are both universal and highly individual.

Grief occurs in stages - yet those stages differ from person to person. How you will express your emotions of grief is not easy to predict. Still, understanding that there are stages of grief will help you better deal with yourself and others at times of change and loss.

Stages of grief

Grieving is like the ebb and flow of the tides rather than a smooth, continual passage. There is no set time period for each stage. Depending on the loss and its significance to you, your grief might be over in a very short period of time or take years to complete. The stages overlap: you can experience a mix of emotions and flip-flop between stages for a while. The stages may happen in a different order or crop up again long after your grief was first experienced and resolved.

The first six months after experiencing a significant loss, such as the death of a spouse, is a critical time. It is important to feel grief and not bottle up or repress emotions. Prolonged depression alters the body's immune system, which increases the risk of illness.

There are several stages of grief which fall into three general categories:

I: **Shock and denial: The "not me" stage**

- **Shock**
  The bottom falls out of the world. Numbness. Disbelief. Denial.

- **Physical changes**
  Alteration of sleeping and eating patterns.

- **Depression**
  Panic. Will I ever recover? Suicide potential.

- **Idealization**
  The past was perfect. The future offers little.

During the shock and denial stage of loss, it is difficult to believe that the loss has happened at all. The person tends to think "Not me! Not me!" He or she may question the lab report or refuse to listen to the truth. There is a denial that the loss has even occurred.

Sometimes that denial is helpful—at least for a brief time. It allows the person a brief respite before having to gear up to deal with the loss.

II. **Guilt, anger and bargaining: The "why me" stage**

- **Guilt**
  How was I involved in the cause of loss? Could I have prevented it?

- **Anger**
  Irrational hostility, expressed or unexpressed. Tears. Cursing.

- **Bargaining**
  What can I do to make the pain go away?

When the fact of the loss can no longer be denied, anger and attempts to bargain away the loss can occur. This is the "Why me?" stage in which the loss is still being pushed away, by blaming someone—the doctor, the deceased person, anyone—for the misfortune. Attempts may be made to erase the loss by promising to take better care of oneself or do more good deeds if only the bad thing can be taken away or undone. Blaming oneself often creates feelings of guilt and despair over what could have been done to prevent the loss.

III. **Adjustment, acceptance and growth: The "get on with it" stage**

- **Realization**
  The past had its faults. The future may not be so bad either.

- **Living with the loss**
  Healthy adjustment. Recognition of the loss. No longer being abnormally disturbed by it.

- **New patterns.**
  By recognizing that the past is behind you, new life patterns develop.

Coming to terms with the loss signifies a time of adjustment and acceptance when there is a feeling of "Well, okay, let's get on with life." Some people get to this stage very quickly. Others may take years to reach this point of reconnection to the outside world.

For many, the acceptance of loss can lead to rapid growth. Even painful change can become a catalyst for self-improvement in physical, mental and spiritual dimensions. The reality of loss can create a new sense of meaning and purpose in you. Look for such opportunities for growth through your own losses and be ready to welcome them.

> *Everyone who loves is vulnerable to the pain of grief, for love means attachment and all human attachments are subject to loss. But grief need not, should not, be a destructive emotion.*
>
> *Joyce Brothers*

A guide through grief*

The first reaction to the death of someone you love is usually emotional as well as physical shock. You simply cannot believe it. Shock is the natural anesthesia which protects you from overwhelming pain. You may experience the need to cry or you may talk in a way others don't understand. Months later you may not remember how you felt or acted during this period.

When the shock wears off, you begin to feel the impact of your grief. You may behave in ways that are unfamiliar to you and unlike your usual self. Difficulty in sleeping, change in appetite, feelings of panic, irritability and apathy are common.

*From Quality Aging Program, Salt Lake County Aging Services, Salt Lake City, Utah

Many widows and widowers suddenly find themselves unable to remember what their partners looked like. At unexpected moments you may find yourself bathed in tears for no obvious reason. Concentration may seem impossible. At times, you may be overcome by exhaustion. Getting out of bed may seem very difficult. It is not unusual for bereaved people to hear familiar sounds associated with the deceased such as footsteps or laughter or a child's cry. People have reported smelling aftershave or perfume associated with the deceased or feeling his or her presence. For many these sensations are comforting. It is important to realize that these and other experiences are perfectly natural grief reactions. They will eventually fade.

An increasing awareness of the loss brings a welling-up of feelings that may be difficult to understand. You may feel helpless, angry, guilty, lonely or relieved. You need time to cry and talk. It takes great courage to risk feeling the depth of the loss.

Loss intensifies feelings of helplessness. You cannot bring the person back and you feel powerless to relieve your pain. Being left by someone close to you is a form of abandonment. Even when death is the cause, anger at that person is a perfectly natural response. It is important to allow yourself to feel honest, painful emotions. Acceptance and expression of your feelings are two of the keys to healing.

Loneliness is often the worst problem for a person whose life partner has died. The loss of being special to this partner can bring about a feeling of emptiness. It is extremely hard to break the habit of having someone to talk to about the day's happenings, family events, what you have read, or anything that may come to mind.

Death many times brings a feeling of relief. Although it is a natural reaction, relief may be difficult to admit. It is important to realize that it does not mean a lack of love for the person who has died. You may feel relieved that the deceased is no longer suffering. Also, many times death frees us from demands, responsibilities and pressures. This is true especially after a long and painful illness.

The passage of time helps to ease the pain of grief. However, time alone is not enough. Expressing your feelings through sound and motion helps mourning. Crying is a healthy emotional outlet; tears are a natural release of tension. You may need to talk endlessly about your loss. Support groups for the bereaved provide a place where you can share your feelings and experiences. You need not be ashamed of your reactions and needs.

Experiencing loss: Your rights and responsibilities

Rights	*Responsibilities*
To have the time you need to deal with your situation.	To not postpone dealing with your loss.
To be unpredictable at first.	To let friends know your moods are not their fault.
To be dealt with honestly.	To speak honestly to others.
To have the support of others.	To let them know your needs.
To make your own decisions.	To seek the information to make the best decisions you can.
To have your individuality respected.	To be your real self.

Helping others at a time of loss

Some people have a natural gift for comforting others at a time of loss. By instinct, they seem to know just what to say or do to ease the pain and provide support. Other people, perhaps the majority, are uncomfortable and unsure of themselves in such situations. Because they do not know the "right thing" to do, they don't do anything—and then feel guilty about that.

You should be assured that any kind of show of concern, sympathy or support is helpful and ultimately appreciated. Follow the suggestions in the guide for helping those in grief on the next page or share your own version of the *Growing Wiser* Support Kit.

> *Friendship doubles our joy and divides our grief.*
> *Anonymous*

Growing Wiser Support Kit

Fill an attractive container— box, basket or bag—with some of the following items to present to a grieving friend:

- *Box of tissue—encourage crying as a good release*

- *A small personal gift—to show you care*

- *A package of soup starter—to make a meal to eat together*

- *Coupons for hugs—good for a free hug anytime, anywhere*

- *Tickets to a movie or concert for you to attend together*

- *Other creative expressions of your caring*

Guide for helping those in grief

Stage	What you can do
Shock and denial	• Send cards or flowers. • Give hugs, hold hands. • Provide food. • Do some chores that need doing (mow the lawn, water the plant, feed the pets, vacuum, clean, etc.). • Provide transportation. • Help the person "see" the evidence of the loss (the x-ray, the wrecked car, etc.). • Expect the person to help with some routine tasks. • Let the person have some time to be alone.
Guilt, anger, bargaining	• Take over a *Growing Wiser* Support Kit. • Listen, listen, listen. Let the person talk as much as he or she wants. • Be together in silence. • Understand and accept abrupt mood shifts. • Help the person learn how to do some new tasks.

Stage	What you can do
Guilt, anger, bargaining (cont'd)	• Provide reassurance that the person was not to blame.
	• Give a plant or pet to be cared for.
	• Recommend and help arrange participation in support groups or with professional counselors if needed.
	• Call or visit frequently.
Adjustment and acceptance	• Provide opportunities for the person to be with you and others.
	• Suggest new activities. Encourage physical activities.
	• Remain accessible as a caring listener if grief returns.
	• Encourage rebuilding of normal ties and tasks.
	• Offer opportunities for play.

Mortal thoughts

A lifespan is that period of time between the twin mysteries of birth and death. No one knows with certainty how long that period will last and what experiences it may hold. To see change as an enemy can rob you of your appreciation of life.

You can rely upon your own strength and resources around you, your friends and family, professional helpers, and your spiritual beliefs. Greet change as a potential friend rather than as a foe. See what you can make of it. Even in preparing for death, you create the opportunity for coming to peace with your life, your life work and those who have been close to you. The approach of death can broaden your perspective and allow you to come to terms with thoughts and feelings that may have troubled you for years.

Personal preparation is also a valuable tool for dealing with your own mortality. A "Living Will" (see next page) can help you exercise control of your life until the very end.

In considering your own life changes, it is helpful to look at both your roots and your legacy. The "Lifeline" (page 86) and "Tree of Life" (page 87) activities will help you see yourself as a part of a continuing process of life. Your contributions and spirit will go on in others long after your passing.

> To resolve your grief you must accept the fact: what was will never be again. You will have to give yourself permission to grieve for it; if you do not, you will never appreciate the future which may be even better or more meaningful than the past.
> *Elisabeth Kubler-Ross*

Recommended Reading

How to Survive the Loss of a Love by Melba Colgrove, et al. New York: Bantam Books, 1976.

Death, The Final Stage of Growth by Elisabeth Kubler-Ross. New York: Prentice-Hall, 1975.

Your Particular Grief by W.E. Oates. Philadelphia: Westminister Press, 1981.

When Bad Things Happen to Good People by Harold S. Kushner. New York: Avon Books, 1981.

Living Will*

If the time comes when I can no longer take part in decisions for my own future, let this statement stand as the testament of my wishes:

If there is no reasonable expectation of my recovery from physical or mental disability, I _____
_____ request that I be allowed to die and not be kept alive by artificial means or heroic measures. Death is as much a reality as birth, growth, maturity and old age—it is the one certainty. I do not fear death as much as I fear the indignity of deterioration, dependence and hopeless pain. I ask that medication be mercifully administered to me for terminal suffering even if it hastens the moment of death. This request is made after careful consideration. Although this document is not legally binding, you who care for me will, I hope, feel morally bound to follow its mandate. I recognize that it places a heavy burden of responsibility upon you, and it is with the intention of sharing that responsibility and of mitigating any feelings of guilt that this statement is made.

(Discuss this document with whoever you think should know your desires, such as family members, close friend, your doctor, your clergyman, your lawyer. When you prepare it, date it, and give copies to those with whom you have discussed it.)

*Information about the Living Will and copies of it may be obtained for free by writing Concern for Dying, 250 W. 57th Street, Room 831, New York, New York 10107.

Lifeline

Drawing your lifeline allows you to chart out the complexities of change and growth in your life. It is a new way to look at your life and let someone else know about you.

Work with a large sheet of paper. If necessary, staple or glue several pieces of typing paper together. You will need three different colored pens or magic markers.

1. Mark the paper along the bottom in 5-year segments beginning at birth.

2. Think about your life in 5-year spans—the ups and down of your life in terms of your physical, emotional and spiritual feelings in each 5-year period. After reminiscing, take the 3 pens and draw a line for each of the three aspects of your life, connecting the ups and downs during each 5-year period.

3. If you wish, fill in the story with drawings, photos, poems, newspaper clippings. Share your lifeline with a friend.

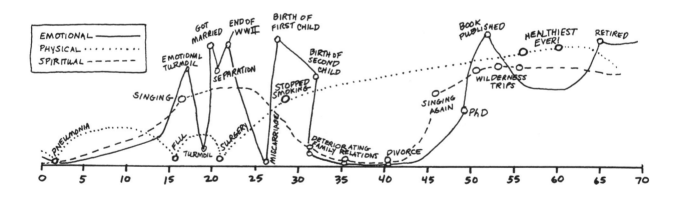

The Tree of Life

They say you only come around once in life. However, your essence lives on in others whose lives you have touched. Similarly there are qualities and traits within you that are a gift from people in your past.

Celebrate the grand composite that is you. One way to do this is through your own *TREE OF LIFE*. On a piece of paper, using as many colors as you like, draw a large tree with many roots, a sturdy trunk and many strong branches.

The roots represent the gift of your forebears—traits such as integrity, willingness to work hard, a love of music—whatever you might have inherited from important people in your past. Write those down. On the trunk list talents and strengths that are uniquely you and that add meaning to your life.

You have influenced many others throughout your life—your children, associates, students, friends, other family members. Throughout the branches jot down characteristics and traits that you have passed on to others—your son's beautiful blue eyes, a love of gardening, and on and on.

When you have finished your *TREE OF LIFE*, savor and enjoy your place in the scheme of things.

Communication

Everything about growing wiser involves communication. The sage within you deserves to be heard and understood. The sage within others deserves equal consideration. In your lifetime you have communicated with thousands of people: family, friends, colleagues, the refrigerator repairman. All individuals come equipped with their own thoughts and feelings, their own perception of what is right and wrong, their own stories. Chances are some of your interactions with your fellow humans have resulted in a communication mix-up.

After his heart attack, Bruce was eager to get back in good health as quickly as possible. Following established policy, he enrolled in a cardiac rehabilitation program designed to monitor the return of heart patients to normal health. One of the nurses assigned to the program counselled Bruce that he could resume normal sexual activity in "four to six weeks."

Three months passed. Bruce became increasingly despondent and withdrawn. He was not making good progress. The nurse challenged Bruce, "Is everything all right at work?" "Yes," came the reply. "How about at home? Is everything okay there?" Another yes. The nurse queried, "What about your sex life? Do you have any problems you wish to discuss?" "What sex life?!", cried Bruce, "You said I couldn't have sex for forty-six weeks and it's killing me!"

We often end up with miscommunication, even when hearing and language are not the causes of the problem. Much of our communication with others is colored by what we value and what we want to hear. It can also be affected by lack of confidence and lack of skill.

Good communication skills are just that — skills. With rare exception, we receive very little training in how to really listen to others or how to genuinely express our hearts and minds. Like all other skills, good communication takes patience, perseverance and heaps of practice. It also takes awareness. If you have ever:

- had difficulty in expressing your feelings,
- felt manipulated into saying "yes" when you want to say "no" (or the other way around!),
- heard "46" when you hoped it would be 4 to 6,

read on—the give and take of good communication awaits you.

Listening

Listening is at the heart of good relationships. When someone really listens to you, you feel appreciated, cared about and understood. When other people do not listen, you feel angry, hurt or snubbed. Misunderstandings arise.

What can you do? How can you make your ears really work for you? Try listening with extra care. There are three kinds of listening skills — each can be highly valuable.

Passive listening and silence

Listening without a verbal response, conveys to the speaker:

- I want to hear what you are saying.

- I accept your feelings.

- You are in charge here.

While silence avoids communication roadblocks and allows the speaker to express feelings, there is no proof that you are really listening. Looking into the speaker's eyes and nodding your head as he or she talks, conveys to the speaker that you are concentrating on his or her words.

Acknowledgment

Using non-commital responses like "oh," "uh-huh," "I see" or responses that convey an invitation, "Would you like to talk about it?" and "I'd like to hear more," lets the speaker know that you are listening and that there is no evaluation or judgment on what is being said.

Active listening

The most effective of the listening skills, active listening "mirrors" or feeds back the speaker's message. It demonstrates that the listener is trying to understand what the other person is communicating.

In active listening, you feed back **only** what the speaker has communicated to you. It is not a time to analyze, give advice, share your feelings or pass judgment. This will enable the speaker to freely express himself/herself and perhaps arrive at a personal solution.

An example of active listening:

Speaker: I'm too old and sick to stay in my own home any longer.
Listener: You feel you are not able to manage your home, so you feel you have to move out.
Speaker: Ever since my husband died, I haven't been able to cope.

Listener:	You feel despair at losing your husband, so you are wondering if you can handle things.
Speaker:	I am very anxious. Everything has changed. I don't know what to do.
Listener:	I sense that you are anxious and unclear about what you should do.
Speaker:	Yes, I do feel unsure and anxious. I had to say it to someone.

Most people, when they are talking about a problem, just want to express their feelings. By actively listening and not offering advice, you allow the speaker to express rather than suppress emotions. Once aired, those feelings often subside. Best of all, being heard and understood results in deeper caring and closer relationships.

> *Skillful listening is the best remedy for loneliness, loquaciousness and laryngitis.*
> *William A. Ward*

Guidelines for using active listening

1. Consider using active listening when:

   - You are free enough of your own concerns and want to help the other person;

   - You are ready to accept another person's feelings or problems.

2. Through listening, help the speaker solve his or her own problem. You won't and can't solve it for him or her.

3. Practice, practice, practice. It will be uncomfortable at first, because it is new. Competence will come with practice.

Whether you listen in silence or with feedback, careful and open listening will give you a tremendous edge in being a good communicator. Effective talking skills will carry you the rest of the way.

> *Listening is not easy. It may be one of the highest arts on earth, and it is a skill that can change our lives.*
> *Gay Gaer Luce*

Have you heard?: Hearing loss and communication

Hearing impairment is a common problem for older adults. About one out of every three people over the age of 65 has some degree of hearing loss. Despite its prevalence, try not to give in to the temptation that "there's nothing to be done about it at my age."

Hearing losses get in the way of good communication. If left untreated and uncorrected, hearing impairments can lead to isolation from important people in your life. What can you do?

- If you have to ask people to repeat themselves more often than you used to, see your doctor. It could be a build up of excess wax in the ear or the side effect of disease or medication or a loss due to other things. Check it out.

- If you have had any ear trouble in the past, get regular check-ups. Early intervention may prevent future disability.

- If you think you need a hearing aid, get one only after expert advice. A hearing aid evaluation will determine which style of hearing aid best suits your needs.

People with hearing losses have to work hard to avoid being isolated. If you are hard of hearing, stick up for yourself. Wear your hearing aid and ask people to speak up if they're mumbling, or lower their voices if they are shouting, or enunciate clearly to help lip-reading.

Assertiveness

To talk well is much more than having a clear, strong speaking voice or being a master of toasts. Effective talking means being able to communicate your ideas, feelings, values and rights. Good talking skills give the sage within you a voice with which to speak.

The best communication skill you can use to feel good about yourself and feel in control of your life is *assertiveness*. Being assertive means speaking up and clearly saying what you want. Assertiveness is when you act in your own best interests, stand up for yourself, and express your opinion and feelings honestly without slighting others. As an assertive person, you exercise your own rights without denying or violating the rights and feelings of others. Being assertive means you value yourself. It means stating your preferences in a way that causes others to take your ideas seriously.

Assertiveness does not guarantee that you will "win" in all situations, but it does make it easier to express yourself. When you express yourself, it is more likely that you will feel good about yourself, be satisfied with the outcome of a situation, and get more of what you need.

The bliss of being forthright! The old, if they are wise, allow themselves this privilege.

Eva Greene

Compare assertiveness with two other talking styles: aggressiveness and passivity.*

Aggressiveness is using hostile words or actions that force others to give in to your own preferences. As an aggressive person, you are interested in "winning," and you attempt to "win" by any means possible, including offending, hurting, or manipulating other people.

Although you may not feel especially anxious and you may "win," the price you pay can be very high. Because you violated the rights of other people, they respond with dislike, hostility, and perhaps aggression toward you. You may find that others are beginning to avoid you and that they react to you sarcastically or with hostility. You may also often find yourself in arguments and left out of the social plans of others.

Passivity is not expressing your own needs, allowing your rights to be ignored, or letting others make decisions for you that you would like to make yourself. It is a wonderful thing to give selflessly to other people. However, this giving should be something you want and choose to do, not something others tell you to do or something you think you should do just to please them.

Passivity may cause you to value yourself less and sometimes feel humiliated. You may feel helpless, controlled, and bitter because you rarely say or get what you want. It is often true that people feel both self-hatred and resentment toward others when they are not expressing themselves assertively.

> *No one can make you feel inferior without your consent.*
> *Eleanor Roosevelt*

Adapted from "The Assertiveness Workshop Manual for Trainers," by C.A. Richey, Seattle: University of Washington, 1979.

Sage, Sherman tank, or doormat?

Read through the statements below and guess if the statement is assertive, aggressive or passive. Remember:

Assertive statements say what you want and express your feelings constructively—like a sage.

Aggressive statements try to get you what you want by bullying, being angry or manipulative—like a Sherman tank.

Passive statements give up on what you want, say you're not important—like a doormat.

1. I hate it when I have to sit around and wait for you every time.

2. It's all right. I don't mind if I don't have any.

3. Please could you move your car. It's blocking my parking space.

4. You snore like a Mack truck and I can't get any sleep!

5. Since I'm their grandmother, I should look after them while my son is on vacation.

6. I'm sorry but I've forgotten your name. Could you please remind me?

Answers: 1,4 Sherman Tank 2,5 Doormat 3,6 Sage

On being assertive

Being assertive and standing up for yourself may not come easily to you. Many people, especially women, have been brought up not to speak their minds, to use politeness and niceness as their primary mode of communication. Being assertive does not mean being hard, cruel or impolite. It simply means being clear about what you want and saying what you mean. It often means negotiating and reaching a compromise. However, the compromise isn't one you're forced into—you agree to it on the basis of what you want.

Your assertiveness rights

You have a right to express your feelings.

You have a right to be treated fairly.

You have a right to live your life as you see fit.

You have the right to decide not to assert yourself.

So what do you do if you are faced with a situation which calls for assertive behavior? How do you stand up for yourself when you see your doctor for a physical, get your car fixed or turn down a request from a family member? Try climbing the Assertiveness Ladder* for preparing an assertive response.

L **Look** at your rights, what you want, and what you need. Define what it is you want and keep it in mind.

A If possible, **arrange** a time and place to discuss the situation.

D **Define** the problem specifically and in easy-to-understand language.

D **Describe** your feelings using "I messages." An "I" message expresses your feelings without blaming others. Say "I'm feeling frustrated" rather than "You frustrate me."

E **Express** your request briefly. Be specific and firm!

R **Reinforce** the possibility of getting what you want by providing the other person with positive incentives to cooperate.

*Assertiveness Ladder adapted from **The Relaxation and Stress Reduction Workbook**, by Davis, Eshelman and McKay, California: New Harbinger Publications, 1980.*

Constructive Criticism*

Suppose you have a very talkative friend whose company you enjoy but whose tendency to interrupt you and others irritates you. What do you do? Ignore the interruptions even though they disturb you? Let slip some scathing remark which may strain the friendship? Vow to befriend only shy introverts? In a situation such as this you may want to give your friend some constructive criticism.

Criticism is something we usually shrink away from—either in giving or receiving. Most of us tend to "swallow" our feelings rather than challenge, correct or criticize someone.

Constructive criticism lets others know that something they are saying or doing is affecting you negatively but without putting the other person down or blaming them. There is a simple three-step process for giving constructive criticism:

When you	do-the-action
I feel	this emotion
I would prefer	suggested alternative.

So to your exuberant, talkative friend you might say:

> When you interrupt me, I feel irritated because you're not listening to me. I would prefer that you let me finish what I was going to say.

By using constructive criticism, you let the other person know a problem exists. You state your feelings without blaming the other person for making you feel that way. You even suggest a remedy for the problem.

Constructive criticism, along with assertiveness, is useful in countless situations. Like all other good communication skills, it lets the sage within you be heard and recognized.

*Adapted from **A Healthy Old Age**, by Stephanie FallCreek and Molly Mettler, New York: Haworth Press, 1984*

Nonverbal communication: Sex and sexuality

A wise man never loses anything if he has himself.
                    Michel de Montaigne

Sex and sexuality communicate a great deal: affection, love, esteem, warmth, sharing, caring, physical, mental, emotional and spiritual bonding. These gifts are not just the province of the "young and in love." Joy in sex and loving knows no age barriers. Almost everyone has the capacity to find lifelong pleasure in sex. To believe in and subscribe to the myth that "old people have no interest in sex" is to miss out on all manner of good things.

As you age, sexual feelings may subside to a degree, but they won't disappear unless you want them to. Your physical and emotional needs change with time and circumstance. Intimacy and sexuality may or may not be important to you. The issue here is one of choice. If you freely decide that sex is no longer right for you, then that is the correct decision. It is possible to live a fulfilling life without sex. However, if you choose to continue enjoying your sexuality, you deserve support and encouragement. You may find, as you age, uncharted sensual territories left to explore.

Sexuality and aging

Age may well offer the opportunity to understand sex as intimate communication in its finest sense.
                    Norman M. Lobsenz.

Sex is like a fine wine; it can improve with age. Growing older may limit some physical actions and activities, but it need not mean losing one of life's great experiences—sharing your sexuality with another.

More and more, healthy older people are realizing that sex can be a fulfilling part of their lives well into their 70's, 80's, and even 90's. There are physical changes which cause some difficulties, but they need not rob the twinkle from your eye.

Age alone does not decrease the pleasure that sex can bring. Some medications (particularly some prescribed for high blood pressure, tranquilizers and some anti-depressants), illness, depression, boredom and excess drinking can all negatively affect sexual activity.

For men, it may take longer to get an erection and the erection may be less firm, but sexual intercourse can still bring joy to both partners. Women may experience irritation during intercourse because of thinning vaginal walls and less vaginal lubrication. A simple solution is to purchase some lubricating jelly (like K-Y jelly). On the other hand, an increase in sexual difficulties may be the result of mental conditioning rather than a physical limitation. If a sexual problem of any origin persists or causes you concern, do ask your doctor for advice.

Physical changes affect some people much more than others, but hardly ever require an end to the enjoyment of sex. Most sexual difficulty is much less likely to crop up if lovemaking is regular. For both men and women, the best way to preserve sexuality is to keep on enjoying it.

Changes in circumstance

Because older people often experience losses which dramatically change their past patterns of sexual expression, they may fall prey to the myth of being sexless. Women and men who have lost their spouses may not know what to do with their sexual feelings. Generally speaking, it is better to take some risks and express your feelings than to suppress them until you no longer are aware that they exist. In almost every case, there is someone near who would enjoy responding.

Desire for sexual expression is no less strong for the single person than for those who are married. Intercourse is not the only way for you to express your sexuality, and sexual enjoyment need not be limited only to ejaculation or orgasm. Touching, embracing and stroking all help to make a person feel secure, loving and loved. The need for such emotional support does not diminish with age. For many older adults, just being around people of the opposite sex has a stimulating effect. It provides an extra dimension which adds to the excitement of life.

Your erogenous mind*: Sexuality need not be physical

Your body can respond sexually to both physical contact with others and to fantasies of contact. Some people might feel that sex is only "real" when it involves the actual touching of a partner. But imaginative images charged with sexual significance have been a source of pleasure for countless persons over the ages.

Your mind can be considered a powerful erogenous zone. Sex consists not only of actions we do with our bodies with a partner or ourselves, it also consists of dreams, daydreams, and other types of fantasies which may not lead to any

*From **Pathways: A Success Guide For A Healthy Life** by D.W. Kemper, J. Giuffre' and G. Drabinski, Boise: Healthwise, Inc., 1985.

visible action but can be inwardly experienced as pleasurable. You must decide what you wish your sexual experience to be. Consider how your sensual experiences either contribute to or detract from your sense of wellbeing.

Sex is only one aspect of the communication that can occur between two people. All communication, including sexuality, is about expressing yourself, feeling good about yourself, being willing to take risks and giving a voice to the sage within you.

> *The basic message of human communication is, "Here I am; there you are. We're not alone."*
> *John K. Lageman*

Recommended Reading

Hearing and the Elderly from the "Age Page" a National Institute on Aging Publication, 1983.

P.E.T. in Action by Dr. Thomas Gordon. New York: Wyden Books, 1976.

Pathways: A Success Guide For A Healthy Life, by Donald W. Kemper, James Giuffre' and Gene Drabinski. Boise, Idaho: Healthwise, Inc., 1985.

Sex After Sixty-five by Norman M. Lobsenz. Public Affairs Pamphlet No. 519. Public Affairs Committee, 1975.

Your Second Life by Gay Gaer Luce. New York: Delacorte Press, 1979.

Sexuality and Aging, by Mona Wasow. Planned Parenthood Publication, 1976.

Disclosure and Discovery

A disclosure is a revelation. Here is a set of questions which may lead you to some revelations and discoveries about yourself.

Have a friend or family member "interview" you using these questions as a guideline. Then switch roles. Remember to use good listening skills.

1. What mark have you imprinted on the world?

2. What is your greatest pride?

3. To what do you attribute your long life?

4. What was the most difficult time of your life?

5. What was the most exciting time of your life?

6. Are you satisfied with life as you have lived it?

A Communication Questionnaire for Parents and Their Adult Children*

Part one: For parents

This exercise is designed to help you understand how well your adult children understand you. Read each of the following statements carefully and write your answer in the space that precedes it. If you agree with the statement, write **yes.** If you disagree with the statement, write **no**.

For the last three questions, fill in the appropriate names. If you like, discuss your answers with your adult children. There are no right or wrong answers. Discussing your point of view may lead to clearer communication between your family's generations.

(Yes or No)

_____ 1. I would rather take advantage of public transportation and community services than rely on my children to provide these things for me.

_____ 2. I would rather live with one of my children and his/her family than live alone.

_____ 3. If I lived with one of my children, I would find it hard to adjust to the noise, activity, and fast pace of the household.

_____ 4. If my children move out of town, I would like to move to be near them.

_____ 5. I think I would be happier in a modern apartment, a senior citizens' complex, or a high-rise condominium than in my present home.

_____ 6. I would like to move to a warmer/cooler/drier climate.

_____ 7. I no longer want to be very active. I am content to spend a lot of time at home alone.

_____ 8. I always enjoy having my children drop in on me, even if they don't call first.

_____ 9. If I become seriously ill and unable to make decisions, I hope my children will use every measure to prolong my life.

(Yes or No)

_____ 10. If I become ill, I would like my children to relieve me of the responsibility of making decisions.

_____ 11. I never want to go into a nursing home.

_____ 12. I think my children should provide me with whatever help I need— even a home, if necessary, so I will not have to move into a nursing home.

_____ 13. If I become unable to care for myself, I would rather move into a nursing home than burden my children with my care.

_____ 14. Personal privacy is very important to me. It would be very difficult for me to accept assistance for bathing, grooming, and personal hygiene.

15. If I ever need help with bathing, grooming, and other personal care, the person I would expect to help is (fill in name) _____ .

16. If I ever need help in managing my money or personal property, the person I would expect to help me is _____ .

17. If I become ill, the person I expect to be my advocate in talking with physicians and other health-care providers is _____ .

*Adapted from a questionnaire developed by Kathy Carroll, Ebenezer Center for Aging and Human Development, Minneapolis, Minnesota.

A Communication Questionnaire for Parents and Their Adult Children*

Part two: For adult children

This exercise is designed to help you understand how well you understand your aging parents(s). Read each of the following statements carefully, then write your answer in the space preceding it. If you agree with the statement, write **yes.** If you disagree with the statement, write **no.** For the last three questions, fill in the appropriate name.

If you like, discuss your answers with your parent(s). There are no right or wrong answers, but discussing your responses can lead to clearer communication between the generations of your family.

(Yes or No)

_____ 1. My parent(s) should take advantage of public transportation and community services instead of relying on me and my family to provide these things.

_____ 2. My parent(s) would be happier living with me and my family than living alone.

_____ 3. My parent(s) would have difficulty adjusting to the noise, activity and fast pace of my household.

_____ 4. If I moved out of town, I would encourage my parent(s) to move to be near me.

_____ 5. My parent(s) would be happier living in a new, modern apartment, a senior citizens' complex, or a high-rise condominium.

_____ 6. My parent(s) would be better off moving to a warmer/cooler/drier climate.

_____ 7. My mother/father no longer wants to be active and involved. She/he is content to spend a lot of time at home alone.

_____ 8. It is all right for me to drop in on my parent(s) at any time, even if I don't call first.

(Yes or No)

_____ 9. If my mother/father could not make the decision, I would ask that every measure be used to prolong her/his life.

_____ 10. If my mother/father becomes frail or ill, I would assume responsibility for making decisions for her/him.

_____ 11. My parent(s) would hate to go to a nursing home, even if professional care became necessary.

_____ 12. I am responsible for giving my parent(s) whatever help is needed—even a home—to avoid nursing home placement.

_____ 13. My parent(s) would be better off selling or giving away some of the heirlooms and personal possessions that take up space and require care.

_____ 14. Personal privacy is important to my parent(s), who would have great difficulty accepting assistance with bathing, grooming, and other personal care.

15. If my parent(s) should ever need help with bathing, grooming, and other personal care, I would expect (fill in name) _____ to help.

16. If my parent(s) ever need help managing money or property, I would expect _____ to help.

17. If my parent(s) should become ill, I would expect _____ to act as an advocate in talking with physicians and other health-care providers.

Adapted from a questionnaire developed by Kathy Carroll, Ebenezer Center for Aging and Human Development, Minneapolis, Minnesota.

Chapter 6

Your World: Home and Beyond

> *May the long time sun shine upon*
> *you*
> *All love surround you*
> *May the clear light within you*
> *Guide you all the way home.*
> *Traditional Blessing*

Growing Wiser is an adventure in mental wellness. It is an "internal" adventure in which you discover the sage within you and explore the riches and wonders of your personal reservoir of wisdom. *Growing Wiser* is also an enterprise which takes you out into the world. The ultimate goal of the adventure is to maintain a sense of personal independence and power for as long as you live. The extent to which you **can** exercise your personal independence and power—the sage within you—is greatly influenced by your environment—be it home, community or the world.

Your environment, the place or places where you live, can have a dramatic effect upon your mental vitality and personal well-being. Imagine for a moment living in an environment that encourages and expects the best out of you as an older citizen. Consider a culture that naturally enhances your wisdom by enabling you to be socially useful, productive and part of a closely-knit community. If you believe that you have that already—terrific—you have created a positive environment for yourself. If you are interested in maintaining that positive environment or in creating one anew, it is time to continue the *Growing Wiser* adventure.

The sage at home

*Be it ever so humble
There's no place like home.
from a song by H.R. Bishop
and J.H. Payne*

At any age, where you live and who and what you have around you help to determine how much you are enjoying life. In short, your "home" is important to your happiness.

After retirement, decisions about your home become more important for two reasons. First, more of your life becomes centered around your home. Second, changes in your needs and interests may make a move seem desirable to you or others.

Perhaps you are already thinking

about a move for any of a host of reasons:

• You may wish to be closer to your children or grandchildren;
• You may want a smaller place;
• You may want a warmer climate;
• You may want to live by the sea or the mountains;
• You may need help keeping up your current house;
• You may wish to live in a safer place;
• You may need a less expensive place to live;
• You may need help with meals, cleaning and personal care;
• You may have always hated your home and at last hope to escape it.

On the other hand, you may find enjoyment in your home and want to remain in it forever. Much of this chapter will cause you to think about your home: what it means to you, what you like about it, what you wish could be improved.

You can have a great deal of control over your home and how well it meets your needs. This chapter will help you consider the options you have for both staying or moving. No matter which you choose, you may consider in what ways your options can be "fine tuned" to add the most to your enjoyment of life.

Making decisions about home

If you are considering a change in your home environment, take lots of time and think it through very carefully. You may even wish to employ the *Growing Wiser* Formula.

Step One:
Understand the facts

The first step in considering decisions about your home is to think about what it truly means to you. How important are each of the following to your enjoyment of home?

Home Factors	Very Important	Important	Not Important
Comfort	_____	_____	_____
Security/Safety	_____	_____	_____
Beauty	_____	_____	_____
Privacy	_____	_____	_____
Freedom to do as you please	_____	_____	_____
Closeness to family	_____	_____	_____
Closeness to friends	_____	_____	_____
Support for meals and personal needs	_____	_____	_____
Convenience to shopping, cultural activities, church	_____	_____	_____
Cost of maintaining your home	_____	_____	_____
Easy maintenance	_____	_____	_____
Access to medical care	_____	_____	_____
Memories (nostalgic value)	_____	_____	_____
Add your own:			
_____	_____	_____	_____
_____	_____	_____	_____
_____	_____	_____	_____

In considering what a "home" means to you, think about how the places you have lived in the past have helped you feel happy and "at home." Next, you can begin applying these factors to your own home and to any other options you are considering. Separate the facts from the myths. Identify those things that are within your control to improve or maintain. For example, if you like where you live but are concerned that you are not eating well and cannot keep your home clean and well-maintained, don't rule out the possibility of someone helping you (possibly for hire, possibly as a kind deed).

Step Two:
Reject unnecessary limitations

Be prepared to reject any limitations which others try to impose on you. ("Mother, you just can't stay in this house by yourself anymore. Even your doctor says you should move in with me.")

Some older adults are limited in their choice of a home. Physical disabilities or health limitations may necessitate a move to a "home" where ambulatory or nursing care is provided. Financial constraints can also pose limitations for either remaining in your own home or finding a new one.

Several options are available to people who wish to remain in their home despite physical and/or finan-cial limitations. The important thing is to maintain control. When making choices for living, be wary of any unnecessary limitations. Call upon the sage within you to maintain control. Use your desire for independence and power to create choices.

Step Three:
Create positive expectations

If you want to live for the rest of your life in a home as nice (or nicer) than you have now, the best thing you can do is to expect your home to be nice. Expect nothing short of a home that fully meets your needs.

Step Four:
Develop an action plan

To make your expectations come about, you may have to take some action. Perhaps the needed action is simply to tell everyone, once and for all, exactly where you want to live and what help you want from them.

Written action plans are always more powerful than vague thoughts about taking action. Review the action plan form on pages 25-27 as a guide for writing your own. In developing your action plan, you may wish to consider the following improvements for making your home more homey.

- Enhance the comfort and aesthetic qualities of your home with plants, flowers, pictures or photographs.

- Arrange to spend more time with close friends by having one or more over for a meal, snack or a talk on a regular basis.

- Post one of your affirmations (page 22) in a location within your home that you will see every day (bathroom mirror, refrigerator).

The challenge is to make choices and plans which encourage independence. Look for ways which will allow you to live where you really want to live, rather than moving just to accommodate your limitations.

Home options for consideration

In developing an action plan you may want to consider these options.

- **Sizing down your home**
Sometimes the size of your home can become a burden. A large house and a large yard may be too difficult to maintain on your own. If the burden, after making whatever changes you can, begins to outweigh your enjoyment of the home, you may consider moving to a smaller home, a condominium, an apartment, or a unit in a senior citizen housing complex.

While such a move is often logical in that it reduces your chore responsibilities and perhaps your

expenses, it also can create problems. Any move tends to break up your support networks with neighbors and service people near your old home. Also, the loss of "the old and familiar" can be an added stress to everyday life. Moving at any age causes stress—yet sometimes such a move may best meet your needs.

- **Home equity conversions**
The single most important financial resource held by the majority of older Americans is the equity they have built up in their homes. Relatively few older homeowners ever use this major asset as a source of income. The vast majority choose to remain in their homes for as long as they can. As a result, most of their financial resources remains tied up in that home. Compared to others, therefore, many older homeowners are asset-rich and income-poor.

If the value of one's home could pay for some home care, more people could afford to purchase it. Until recently, however, the only way to use the savings tied up in a home was to sell and leave the home, and then purchase the care in a new setting.

Within the past few years, a variety of approaches have been developed for cashing in on some of the equity in a home without having to move out of it. The purpose of these "home equity conversion" plans is to enable older persons to convert part of their home equity into income while they remain in the home. Ask your banker, lawyer or a reliable real estate professional for more information about Home Equity Conversions.

Interdependent living: Living with others

Many older people reach a decision to move not only to a smaller home but to one with special opportunities for developing interdependence with other people. Such options for interdependent living include:

- **Retirement communities**
  Usually self-contained, retirement communities offer leisure living with other older adults.

- **Home sharing**
  Many older adults are opening their homes to others for companionship or in exchange for providing needed home or personal care services, or for help with finances. Although many home-sharing programs involve just older adults, intergenerational arrangements are also becoming common.

- **Granny flats**
  Small, detached houses on the property of adult children allow older adults to maintain their independence while living near their families.

Special support for independent living

When a problem arises which threatens your ability to live where you wish, look for the support options that address the problem with the least impact on your independence. Consider the following list of "living support options."* You may wish to share this list with your family and your doctor prior to making decisions concerning your living arrangements. (While you may need some extra support and services during a period of illness, try not to use a service longer than you really need it. You goal should be to maintain a sense of control and independence.)

Concerns	Support Options
Food and meal preparations Difficulty cooking meals, shopping for food, and arranging a nutritious diet	**Home-delivered meals** "Meals-on-Wheels" delivers to your home, sliding fees **Nutrition sites** meals served at senior centers, churches, schools, and other sites **Cooperatives** arrangements with neighbors to exchange a service for meals, food shopping, etc. **Shared Meals** with friends, neighbors or relatives.
Personal care Help needed to bathe, to dress or to do other routine activities	**Home Aides** from private agencies listed in the phone book **Home sharing** sharing the home with another person who is willing to provide this kind of assistance in exchange for room and board

*Adapted from the Manual on Psychosocial Issues and Community Resources for the Elderly, University of Washington Long Term Care Gerontology Center, 1982.

Concerns	Support options
Fear of accidents Fear of having an accidental injury or illness without access to assistance	**Telephone reassurance services** through local hospitals or friends, neighbors or relatives **Postal alert** register with your local senior center. A sticker on your mail box alerts the letter carrier to check for accumulation of mail. **Prevention** check out your home for safety. Move to downstairs bedroom. Remove throw rugs. Install grips in bathrooms and rails on steps. **Buddy system** regularly check on each other at certain times
Isolation Loneliness or boredom in living alone	**Senior centers** provide social opportunities, volunteer opportunities, outings **Church or parks department-sponsored clubs** social activities, volunteer opportunities, outings **Support groups** for widows, stroke victims, and others in need of general support.
Transportation Difficulty in arranging transportation to medical appointments, shopping, recreation, etc.	**Carpools** with neighbors, families or other older people, fellow volunteers or workers

Concerns	Support options
Transportation (continued)	**City provisions for older people** reduced bus fares, taxi cab scrip
	Volunteer services Red Cross, Salvation Army, church organizations for emergency or occasional transportation
Financial concerns Difficulty managing financial affairs because of poor eyesight or other problems	**Authorization of second signature** with a relative or friend for ease of paying bills
	Volunteer assistance available from the Red Cross, Salvation Army, church groups, senior centers, senior outreach services.
	Power of attorney given to relative or friend for handling financial matters
Ability to afford your mortgage and home maintenance costs	**Home equity conversion plan** (see page 111)
Nursing care Need for occasional nursing care	**Visiting nurse** services provided through Medicare/Medicaid, private insurance, or sliding scale fees
	Veteran's Administration Hospital home care for veterans over 60 years old for specific situations
	Private-duty nurse many nurses work independently or through private agencies.

Shelter and care alternatives

If, at some point, you need lots of extra help, you might consider living in a retirement center with shelter care and nursing care facilities. Such centers allow you to remain as independent as possible while having medical and personal care support close by, should you need it.

Living with an adult child is also a viable alternative. Certainly, many more older adults live with their children than live in nursing and shelter homes. A relationship of interdependence can develop in which the older adult contributes as much needed support to the family as he or she receives from them.

"There's no place like home" for the sage. Whether you make your home in a house, an apartment, a retirement community or a care facility, be sure that it reflects you. Create an environment in which you are the chief executive officer, free to maintain control, and to exercise personal independence and power.

Beyond the home: The sage with others

People who need people are the luckiest people in the world.
from a song by Bob Merrill and Jule Styne

People need people to be physically healthy and mentally vital. Living without close friends and relationships has been determined to be hazardous to your health.* It's true, people with strong ties with other people have a fifty percent lower death rate than those with few social ties. They also suffer less illness and have higher general levels of health.

What does this mean to you? Basically, it means that if you have around you close family and friends who care about you and whom you care about, it will be easier for you to stay physically healthy and mentally vital.

Before making any decisions about where you want to live, think about what effect your choice might have on those with whom you spend time. The quality of your relationships may be the most important factor in both how long you live and how well you live—your quality of life. Just having people that you like around you helps you recover more quickly from illness and lessens your

*Based on a 9-year study by Berkman and Syme of 7,000 residents of Alameda County, California.

chances for diseases ranging from arthritis to depression.

You may differ quite a bit from others in your need for companionship. For some people, a single intimate relationship (a marriage for example) is all that is needed for social support. For others, church groups, friends, children, clubs and community activities can all contribute to strong social support. Even the care and ownership of a pet has been shown to help people stay healthy. As any dog lover or cat lover knows, pets both rely on you and give you support.

How does social support help you remain healthy and vital? Perhaps over time, your perceived sense of support from others leads you to a greater sense of control over your own life. This sense of control and confidence could explain the dramatic role of close social ties in maintaining mental vitality.

Social ties that you maintain with other individuals, groups and your community provide a web which seems to assure that every person in it receives a certain amount of emotional and physical support. With strong support from friends, even people who experience major losses do not suffer to the same extent as more isolated individuals. Close, confiding personal relationships have been found to reduce or buffer stress connected with major life-change events.

Nurturing your network of support

The people around you are a major part of the solution to maintaining mental vitality and a positive sense of well-being. If you have taken the "all your eggs in one basket" approach to support by limiting your important relationships to only one person, you may find yourself in trouble if that person should die, move away or become very ill. At those times, strong friendships and common bonds with others will be important aids in refocusing your life to enjoy the years ahead. What follows are some suggestions for nurturing your social networks:

1. Begin by enriching your existing personal relationships.

    • Tell your closest friends how much their friendship means to you.

    • Arrange to meet with close friends on a regular basis. Don't just wait for celebration or crisis to bring you together.

    • Consider the support you get or might get from church groups, senior center activities or clubs in which you participate. Support gained and shared with people in these settings is often there for the asking.

2. Extend your friendships and support network.

- It is never too late to make and enjoy new friends. Look for them everywhere. Enroll in a class, join a group, or go on a tour. There are plenty of potential friends out there. It is up to you to find them.

- Consider getting support from others who share your concerns or interests. There are groups for just about every one including widows and widowers, stroke victims, singles, dancers, walkers, swimmers, diabetics, dieters and computer buffs. Ask you senior center for a list of local groups.

- Create your own support group if those that are available aren't to your liking.

Part of growing wiser is the recognition that people can and do help others. By adding new friends you not only help them and yourself, but you create a healthier environment for your entire community.

A friend is a present you give yourself.
Robert Louis Stevenson

The sage in his/her community

Becoming involved in community affairs will not only do wonders for expanding your social support network, it can also work miracles for other older adults. Consider the wealth of experience and knowledge you can bring to committees, councils, and legislative bodies which are involved with shaping the future of your community. You can bring an older adult's perspective, a perspective that is most often conspicuous by its absence. Your participation at the planning level in community decisions will not only affect the decision at hand, but more importantly it will help others, particularly younger people, appreciate the valuable contributions elders can make within their community.

Call your mayor's office and county commissioner's office to get a list of the decision-making and advisory bodies that are crying out for citizen participation. Pick one that interests you and use the sage within to reach out. Reach out to make your community better for you, for other older adults, and for all those who share in the pride of your community.

The sage in the world

> *One sees a flame in the eyes of the young, but in the eyes of the old, one sees light.*
>
> *Victor Hugo*

The world has always had its problems. War, hunger, poverty and calamity have been present throughout history. They remain a challenge today. Added to these age-old concerns are more recent worries about environmental decay and nuclear destruction.

More than anything else, the world needs wisdom. Only through wisdom can society learn from the past to avoid problems of the future. The world's best chance to gain that wisdom and perspective is through its older people. In many cultures, the elders of the community are relied upon to guide their people through the challenges and opportunities before them. There is even greater need for this today.

Every wise person can make significant contributions to the resolution of problems. Your challenge is to focus your wisdom on those issues for which you have great concern. By expressing your concern from the perspective of a sage, you and others can steer society and its leaders toward workable solutions. Turn to the sage within you and ask how you and your wisdom can contribute to making the world a better place.

Dispelling ageism

As important as the wisdom of age and experience is to the solution of today's problems, there are many forces working against it. *Ageism* is discrimination against older people. It is often unintentional and sometimes almost unconscious. A store clerk may try to talk to you as if you were a child. Younger people may seem to ignore you at a party or have no interest in what you have to say. You may feel you are being looked at as "just another old fool." Such ageism, no matter how innocent, can rob you of personal power and rob the world of what you have to offer. Don't allow it to happen to you. Speak up for your rights and your interests in a way that shows the sage within you. Use the assertiveness skills discussed on pages 95-96 and the *Growing Wiser* Formula to dispel ageism whenever it crosses your path.

Ambassadors of wisdom

Some people strengthen society just by being the kind of people they are.

John W. Gardner

The best way to help restore wisdom to the world is to act like a sage wherever you go. Consider yourself to be an ambassador of wisdom. Without pushing your opinions on others, make it known that you look at the issues with a very broad perspective. To the degree that you and other elders begin to respect your own wisdom and to express it, the rest of society will begin to accept and rely on that wisdom.

Older people worldwide, through their wisdom and experience, share an increased understanding and a broader perspective. However, the recognition and acceptance of this wisdom varies from culture to culture. Perhaps greater world unity can be achieved by respecting and honoring the wisdom that develops in the later years of life. As the world becomes smaller through faster travel and improved communication, there is an opportunity for older people everywhere to join together. It is not too late for the whole world to start *Growing Wiser.*

Go in search of yourself
Love yourself and others
Learn from yourself and others
Plan with yourself and others
Serve yourself and with others
Begin with what you have
And build on what you are.

Chinese poem

Recommended Reading

The Art of Aging by Evelyn Mandel. Minneapolis: Winston Press, 1981.

A Practical Guide to Independent Living for Older People by H.H. Phillips and C.K. Roman. Seattle: Pacific Search Press, 1984.

Growing Older, Growing Better by Jane Porcino, Reading, MA: Addison-Wesley, 1983.

You and Your Aging Parent by Barbara Silverstone and Helen K Hyman. New York: Pantheon Books, 1982.

Index

Index